◆ THE FLAVORS OF ◆
BON APPÉTIT

◆ THE FLAVORS OF ◆
BON APPÉTIT
◆ 1996 ◆

from the Editors of Bon Appétit

Condé Nast Books ◆ Pantheon
New York

For *Condé Nast* Books

Jill Cohen, *President*
Ellen Maria Bruzelius, *Direct Marketing Director*
Lucille Friedman, *Fulfillment Manager*
Patricia Van Note, *Product Development Manager*
Tom Downing, *Direct Marketing Manager*
Jennifer Metz, *Direct Marketing Associate*
John Crutchfield, *Direct Marketing Assistant*

For *Bon Appétit* Magazine

William J. Garry, *Editor-in-Chief*
Laurie Glenn Buckle, *Editor, Bon Appétit Books*
Marcy MacDonald, *Editorial Business Manager*
John Hartung, *Editorial Production Director*
Sybil Shimazu Neubauer, *Editorial Coordinator*
Marcia Lewis, *Editorial Support*
Angeline Vogl, *Supplemental Text*
Norman Kolpas, *Supplemental Text*
Jennifer Rylaarsdam, *Research*

Produced in association with Patrick Filley Associates, Inc.
Designed by Laura Hammond Hough

Front Jacket: Garden Vegetable Lasagne (page 116).

Back Jacket: Chicken Salad with Greens, Roasted Potatoes and Shallots (page 81);
Chocolate Raspberry Tart (page 174); Spicy Garbanzo and Turkey Sausage Soup (page 28).

Contents Page: Top: Pasta with Lobster, Tomatoes and "Herbes de Maquis" (page 130);
Lower Left: Grilled Vegetable Tostadas with Two Salsas (page 108);
Lower Right: Frozen Framboise Mousse with Apricot Sauce and Raspberries (page 207).

ISBN 0-679-44236-7

Manufactured in the United States of America

FIRST EDITION

2 4 6 8 9 7 5 3 1

◆ Contents ◆

◆Introduction◆

If you leaf through a year of *Bon Appétit*, you will notice that certain words appear frequently — words like *favorite, classic, finest* and *best*. And while we at the magazine admit to using these superlatives often, we don't use them lightly.

Issue after issue, we strive to bring you truly outstanding recipes, those that pass all our tests with flying colors and meet specific criteria in terms of originality, appearance, texture and, of course, taste. The result is a magazine filled with recipes we have no qualms about describing with superlatives.

Over the course of a year, though, some recipes make even more lasting impressions — on us, the editors, on our writers, on chefs and on you, our readers. They're the recipes we find ourselves cooking at home; they're the ones that we see on menus in restaurants across the country; and they're the ones that move you to write us in thanks. You might call them "the best of the best."

More than 200 of these special recipes make up this third collection of *The Flavors of Bon Appétit*. It's a wonderfully varied group. You will find recipes for every course; recipes from Asia, the Mediterranean and your own backyard; recipes both simple and sophisticated; recipes for healthy meals and special-occasion indulgences. For all their variety, though, these recipes share one common — or rather, uncommon — characteristic: They are well worthy of being labelled "the best."

·Starters·

The best first courses, however simple or elaborate, beguile the appetite, offering exciting tastes and intriguing textures of their own as they build anticipation for the main course to come. As the outstanding recipes that follow demonstrate, such goals can be achieved in many ways.

Finger foods, such as Asparagus and Prosciutto Bundles (page 11), can set a festive tone for a dinner party, particularly when accompanied by something exotic to drink, like the Mango-Banana Daiquiris (page 37) or the Margaritas with Tropical Fruit (page 36). A classic sit-down appetizer, such as Artichokes with Goat Cheese (page 19) or Crab Salad with Endive and Tomato-Cilantro Sauce (page 23), commences a meal in a more stately manner. When you want to strike a comforting note, consider beginning with soup, whether robust and satisfying, like Spicy Garbanzo Bean and Turkey Sausage Soup (page 28); rich and elegant, like Spinach Bisque with Sour Cream (page 25); or cool and refreshing, like Cucumber-Yogurt Soup (page 26).

As you consider such appealing starters, you may well be tempted to look no further for your menu selections. Feel free to follow a popular dining trend, enjoying an entire meal composed of fabulous first courses alone.

Spicy Garbanzo Bean and Turkey Sausage Soup, page 28.

Beef Tenderloin and Artichoke Puree on Rye Toasts

◆ ◆ ◆

1	14-ounce can artichoke hearts, drained well
3	tablespoons mayonnaise
3	tablespoons freshly grated Parmesan cheese
1	tablespoon fresh lemon juice
2	teaspoons chopped fresh tarragon or ¾ teaspoon dried
1	teaspoon grated lemon peel
1	garlic clove, minced
¼	teaspoon ground nutmeg
	Generous pinch of cayenne pepper
2	teaspoons vegetable oil
2	8-ounce beef tenderloin steaks (each about 1 inch thick)
48	slices cocktail rye bread
48	small arugula leaves
	Thinly shaved Parmesan cheese

Puree artichokes in processor until almost smooth. Add mayonnaise, grated Parmesan, lemon juice, tarragon, lemon peel, garlic, nutmeg and cayenne. Process until well blended. Transfer to small bowl. Season with salt and pepper.

Heat oil in heavy large skillet over medium-high heat. Season steaks with salt and pepper. Add to skillet and cook to desired doneness, about 5 minutes per side for medium-rare. Transfer to plate. Cool. *(Artichoke puree and steaks can be made 1 day ahead. Cover separately and refrigerate.)*

Preheat oven to 350°F. Using 1½-inch round cookie cutter, cut 48 rounds from rye bread. Arrange rounds on large baking sheet. Bake until golden brown, about 8 minutes. Cool.

Spread 1 teaspoon artichoke puree on each rye round (save remaining puree for another use). Top with arugula leaf. Cut each steak across grain into 24 thin strips. Starting at 1 short end, roll up each beef strip. Place atop arugula. Garnish with shaved Parmesan.

MAKES 48

◆ ◆ ◆

The artichoke puree in this appetizer (shown at right with the asparagus bundles) has a nice tarragon flavor that is a lovely complement to the beef. Use the remaining puree as a dip for crudités or wedges of pita bread.

◆ ◆ ◆

Asparagus and Prosciutto Bundles

◆ ◆ ◆

48 thin asparagus spears

2½ ounces soft fresh goat cheese (such as Montrachet),
room temperature

2 tablespoons chopped fresh basil

1 tablespoon toasted pine nuts, chopped

1 tablespoon water

1 teaspoon grated orange peel

2 ounces thinly sliced prosciutto, cut into twenty-four 4 x 1-inch strips

Cut stalks from asparagus, leaving 2-inch-long tips. (Reserve stalks for another use.) Cook asparagus tips in large pot of boiling salted water until just crisp-tender, about 1 minute. Drain asparagus. Transfer asparagus to paper towels and then drain well.

Mix goat cheese, basil, pine nuts, water and orange peel in small bowl to blend. Season with salt and pepper. Spread scant 1 teaspoon filling over each prosciutto strip. Arrange 2 asparagus tips atop filling at 1 short end of prosciutto. Roll up prosciutto, enclosing base of asparagus. Press to seal. Place on platter. *(Can be made 1 day ahead. Cover and refrigerate.)*

MAKES 24

If there are food marriages made in heaven, then prosciutto and melon are surely one of them. The melon, usually cantaloupe, just seems to bring out the best in the rich, salty, silky ham. And if you ask connoisseurs, chances are they'll tell you the best prosciutto comes not from this country, but from Parma, in the Emilia-Romagna region southeast of Milan. There, the pigs are fed on grain and the whey from the region's Parmigiano-Reggiano cheese, as they have been for two thousand years.

Prosciutto is made from raw pork leg that is salt-cured and air-dried, a process that destroys the dangerous organisms often associated with raw pork. While precise methods and curing times vary, a Parma prosciutto typically takes about 400 days to cure. The final product will also vary—in flavor, color and texture—depending on the type of hog and where it was processed. In general, though, the imported prosciutto tends to be saltier and has a deeper color than the domestic version.

◆ ◆ ◆

Yogurt "Cheese" with Pita and Olives

♦ ♦ ♦

Cheesecloth

4 cups plain yogurt (do not use low-fat or nonfat)

1 teaspoon sesame seeds

½ teaspoon salt

¼ teaspoon dried summer savory

⅛ teaspoon cayenne pepper

⅛ teaspoon ground cumin

2 tablespoons extra-virgin olive oil

Toasted pita bread triangles

Assorted olives

Set strainer over large bowl. Line strainer with 4 layers of cheesecloth, allowing 4 inches to extend over sides of strainer (do not let strainer touch bottom of bowl). Spoon yogurt into strainer. Gather cheesecloth together; fold over yogurt. Refrigerate at least 8 hours or overnight (liquid will drain out and yogurt will thicken).

Combine sesame seeds, salt, summer savory, cayenne and

♦ ♦ ♦

This tangy, fresh yogurt "cheese" vies for attention with hummus and tahini on the standard Israeli platter of *mezze*, or appetizers. Here it's seasoned with sesame seeds and spices, and drizzled with olive oil. Plan to start this appetizer (pictured at right with the Grilled Ground Lamb Kebabs with Fresh Hot-Pepper Paste from page 58) the day before serving.

♦ ♦ ♦

cumin in small bowl. Open cheesecloth at top. Using rubber spatula, transfer drained yogurt to bowl. Drizzle olive oil over. Sprinkle with sesame seed mixture. Place bowl in center of platter; surround with pita bread triangles and olives.

MAKES ABOUT 2 CUPS

Blanketed Eggplant

◆ ◆ ◆

8 small Japanese eggplants, peeled
16 large fresh mint leaves
4 large garlic cloves, 2 slivered, 2 flattened

2 cups olive oil (for deep frying)

2 pounds tomatoes

7 tablespoons extra-virgin olive oil
1 medium onion, chopped
6 fresh basil leaves
1 tablespoon dried oregano

1½ tablespoons drained capers

Place eggplants on double thickness of paper towels. Salt generously. Let stand 1 hour. Pat dry with paper towels. Cut 2 deep incisions in each eggplant. Using tip of knife, push 1 mint leaf and 1 garlic sliver into each incision.

Pour 2 cups oil into heavy medium saucepan and heat to 375°F. Add eggplants in batches and fry until deep golden brown, turning occasionally, about 4 minutes. Transfer eggplants to paper towels and drain thoroughly.

Blanch tomatoes in boiling water for 20 seconds. Drain. Peel tomatoes. Cut tomatoes in half; squeeze out seeds. Chop tomatoes.

Heat 4 tablespoons extra-virgin olive oil in large pot over high heat. Add 2 flattened garlic cloves; sauté until light brown, about 3 minutes. Discard garlic. Add onion; sauté until translucent, about 5 minutes. Add tomatoes, basil and oregano. Simmer until thick and reduced to 3 cups, stirring occasionally, about 20 minutes.

Mix capers and 3 tablespoons olive oil into sauce. Season with salt and pepper. Reduce heat. Add eggplants. Simmer 5 minutes, spooning sauce over eggplants occasionally. Spoon sauce onto platter. Top with eggplants. Serve warm or at room temperature.

4 SERVINGS

◆ ◆ ◆

In this authentically Sicilian dish, a caper-flavored tomato sauce "blankets" whole, fried Japanese eggplants. The appetizer can be served warm or at room temperature.

◆ ◆ ◆

Mushroom-Ham Brochettes

◆ ◆ ◆

6   tablespoons mayonnaise
2   large garlic cloves, pressed
1   teaspoon fresh lemon juice
1   teaspoon plus 3 tablespoons extra-virgin olive oil

¼   pound ⅛-inch-thick slices serrano ham or prosciutto,
     cut into thirty 1-inch squares
24   small mushrooms, stems removed
6   6- to 8-inch bamboo skewers

Coarse salt

Whisk mayonnaise, garlic, lemon juice and 1 teaspoon oil in small bowl to blend. Season with salt and pepper.

Alternate 5 ham squares and 4 mushrooms on each skewer. Brush skewers with 2 tablespoons oil. *(Garlic mayonnaise and skewers can be made 6 hours ahead. Cover separately and chill.)*

Brush heavy large skillet with remaining 1 tablespoon oil; heat over medium heat. Add skewers and cook until mushrooms are brown and softened, turning occasionally, about 12 minutes. Season skewers with salt. Serve, passing garlic mayonnaise separately.

6 SERVINGS

Garlic Shrimp

◆ ◆ ◆

8   ounces uncooked large shrimp, peeled, deveined
1   teaspoon coarse salt

¼   cup olive oil
1   tablespoon chopped garlic
1   small bay leaf
1   1-inch piece dried red chili pepper, seeded
1   tablespoon minced fresh parsley

Place shrimp in bowl; sprinkle with coarse salt and toss. Let stand at room temperature 15 minutes.

Heat oil in medium skillet over high heat. Add garlic, bay leaf and dried pepper and stir 1 minute. Add shrimp; stir until just cooked through, 3 minutes. Transfer to dish. Sprinkle with parsley.

4 SERVINGS

Layered Potato Salad with Tuna

◆ ◆ ◆

2   pounds medium-size red-skinned potatoes

6   tablespoons flaked drained canned white meat tuna
1½   teaspoons plus 2 tablespoons white wine vinegar
6   ·tablespoons extra-virgin olive oil
3   hard-boiled eggs, peeled

⅓   cup thinly sliced onion
2   tablespoons minced fresh parsley

Cook potatoes in large pot of boiling salted water until tender, about 35 minutes. Cool. Peel and cut into ¼-inch-thick rounds.

Combine tuna and 1½ teaspoons vinegar in small bowl. Whisk oil and remaining 2 tablespoons vinegar in another small bowl; add 1 hard-boiled egg yolk and mash. Season vinaigrette with salt and pepper. *(Potatoes, tuna and vinaigrette can be made 6 hours ahead. Cover separately; chill. Rewhisk vinaigrette before continuing.)*

Thinly slice remaining 2 eggs and 1 egg white. Arrange half of potato slices in shallow dish. Season with salt and pepper. Top with half of onion, tuna, egg and parsley. Drizzle half of vinaigrette over. Repeat layering with remaining potato slices, salt and pepper, onion, tuna, egg and parsley. Drizzle remaining vinaigrette over. Serve at room temperature or chill until serving time.

6 SERVINGS

◆ ◆ ◆

This delicious tapa, or appetizer, is called *flamenquines* in Spanish. The precise origin of the name is unknown, but it is most certainly related to the term *flamenco*, which refers to any colorful dish native to the region of Andalusia.

◆ ◆ ◆

Andalusian Pork Rolls

◆ ◆ ◆

2   tablespoons minced fresh parsley
2   garlic cloves, minced
6   ½-inch-thick boneless pork loin chops (about 3 ounces each)
6   thin slices serrano ham or prosciutto (about 2 ounces)
2   large eggs, lightly beaten with 2 teaspoons milk
1   cup (about) plain dried breadcrumbs

    Olive oil (for frying)

Mix parsley and garlic in small bowl. Place pork between 2 sheets of waxed paper. Using mallet, pound pork to ¼-inch thickness. Cut each pork cutlet into 5 x 3-inch rectangle. Top each with 1 ham slice. Sprinkle with parsley mixture. Starting at short end, roll up each cutlet; secure with toothpicks. Dip pork rolls into egg mixture, then coat with breadcrumbs.

Pour oil into deep medium skillet to depth of 1 inch and heat to 375°F. Add pork rolls and fry until golden and cooked through, about 13 minutes. Drain on paper towels. Cut rolls crosswise into ¾-inch-wide slices. Serve immediately.

6 SERVINGS

Split Pea Puree

◆ ◆ ◆

¼   cup olive oil
1   cup chopped onion
6½ cups water
1¾ cups split peas (about 12 ounces)

Capers

Heat oil in heavy large Dutch oven over medium heat. Add 1 cup chopped onion; sauté 5 minutes. Add water and split peas. Bring to boil. Reduce heat. Cover; simmer until peas are very soft and falling apart, stirring occasionally, about 50 minutes. Uncover; simmer until very thick and reduced to 4 cups, stirring often, about 1 hour. Season with salt and pepper. *(Can be made 1 day ahead. Cover and refrigerate. Bring to room temperature or rewarm over low heat, stirring frequently, before serving.)*

Serve warm or at room temperature sprinkled with capers.

MAKES ABOUT 4 CUPS

◆ ◆ ◆

Capers make a simple garnish for this luscious dip made from pureed split peas. It's also good garnished with crumbled feta cheese, chopped onion and herbs. Accompany it with hunks of feta cheese, caper berries, olives and assorted breads.

◆ ◆ ◆

Shrimp in Grape Leaves

◆ ◆ ◆

6   tablespoons chopped fresh parsley

8   garlic cloves, minced

1   8-ounce jar grape leaves,* drained

24 extra-large uncooked shrimp (about 12 ounces), peeled, deveined
     Olive oil

8   bamboo skewers, soaked in water 30 minutes

Combine parsley and garlic in small bowl. Blanch 24 grape leaves in pot of boiling water 1 minute. Drain. Rinse under cold water. Drain well. Place grape leaf, veined side up, on work surface. Cut off stem. Brush shrimp with olive oil. Place shrimp at center of bottom edge of grape leaf. Sprinkle 1 teaspoon parsley mixture over shrimp. Fold sides of grape leaf over shrimp, then roll up, enclosing shrimp completely. Repeat with remaining leaves, shrimp and parsley mixture. Thread 3 shrimp packages on each skewer. *(Can be prepared 1 day ahead. Cover and chill.)*

Prepare barbecue (medium-high heat) or preheat broiler. Brush shrimp packages lightly with oil. Grill or broil skewers until shrimp are cooked through, about 3 minutes per side. Serve shrimp warm or at room temperature.

*Grape leaves are available at Greek, Middle Eastern and Italian markets and some supermarkets.

MAKES 24

◆ ◆ ◆

In this delicious appetizer, shrimp are wrapped in grape leaves, skewered and grilled. In Greece, the leaves are used to wrap everything from little game birds to small whole fish, but most often in that ubiquitous local treat, dolmades.

◆ ◆ ◆

Artichokes with Goat Cheese

◆ ◆ ◆

8   tablespoons fresh lemon juice
6   medium artichokes, tops and stems trimmed

8   ounces soft fresh goat cheese (such as Montrachet)
3   tablespoons whipping cream
3   teaspoons minced fresh thyme or 1 teaspoon dried
2   large garlic cloves, pressed

3   tablespoons butter
3   tablespoons olive oil

Bring large pot of water to boil. Add 2 tablespoons lemon juice to water. Add artichokes and cook until tender, about 25 minutes. Drain well. Cool completely. Using small spoon and keeping artichokes intact, carefully remove tiny center leaves and chokes.

Mix goat cheese, cream, 2 teaspoons thyme and garlic in small bowl. Season to taste with salt and pepper. Spoon mixture into center of artichokes, dividing equally. Place each artichoke in center of square piece of foil large enough to cover artichoke completely. Gather foil up around artichoke, twisting top of foil to secure. *(Can be prepared 1 day ahead. Refrigerate.)*

Preheat oven to 400°F. Place artichokes on baking sheet and bake until heated through, about 15 minutes. Melt butter in heavy small skillet. Add olive oil and remaining 6 tablespoons lemon juice and bring to simmer. Remove from heat and stir in remaining 1 teaspoon thyme. Season to taste with salt and pepper. Unwrap artichokes. Place each in center of plate. Drizzle butter mixture around each artichoke and serve immediately.

6 SERVINGS

Seared Sea Scallops with Crème Fraîche and Caviar

◆ ◆ ◆

1   teaspoon vegetable oil
12   large sea scallops, cut horizontally into 2 rounds

¼   cup crème fraîche or sour cream
½   ounce caviar
4   fresh chives, cut into 1-inch lengths

Heat oil in large nonstick skillet over medium-high heat. Season scallops with salt and pepper. Cook scallops until golden on bottom, about 2 minutes. Turn over; sauté until just cooked through, about 1 minute. Drain on paper towels. Cool to room temperature.

Top each scallop with ½ teaspoon crème fraîche. Top with caviar. Garnish with chives and serve.

MAKES 24

Grapes marinated in Port with rosemary and then combined with the mild garlic and the creamy cheese lead to an inventive appetizer (pictured above with the seared scallops).

◆ ◆ ◆

Roasted Garlic, Brie and Grape Crostini

◆ ◆ ◆

30   garlic cloves, peeled
½   cup olive oil
¾   teaspoon ground thyme

1½   cups seedless grapes, halved
¼   cup ruby Port
1   teaspoon chopped fresh rosemary
1   baguette, cut diagonally into 24 slices, toasted
8   ounces Brie cheese, rind removed, room temperature
     Fresh rosemary sprigs

Preheat oven to 325°F. Combine garlic and oil in small baking dish. Bake until garlic is tender, about 20 minutes. Drain, reserving 3 tablespoons oil. Transfer garlic to processor. Add thyme and reserved oil; puree. *(Can be made 1 day ahead. Chill. Bring to room temperature before using.)*

Mix grapes, Port and 1 teaspoon rosemary in bowl. Let stand 15 minutes. Spread each toast slice with 1 teaspoon garlic. Spread 2 teaspoons Brie over. Top with grapes and herb sprigs.

MAKES 24

Leeks Vinaigrette with
Red Bell Pepper and Mint

◆ ◆ ◆

1	medium red bell pepper
4	medium leeks (white and pale green parts only)
4	teaspoons red wine vinegar
2	teaspoons Dijon mustard
3	tablespoons olive oil
½	cup crumbled feta cheese
⅓	cup coarsely chopped walnuts, toasted
2	tablespoons chopped fresh mint

Char bell pepper over gas flame or under broiler until blackened on all sides. Seal in paper bag and let stand 10 minutes. Peel, seed and chop pepper. Set aside.

Cut leeks in half lengthwise to within 1 inch of base, leaving base intact. Rinse leeks under running water. Add leeks to pot of boiling salted water; reduce heat and simmer until leeks are tender when pierced with knife, about 7 minutes. Drain; cool completely. Using paper towels, squeeze excess moisture from leeks. Cut leeks completely in half lengthwise. Cut off and discard roots. Cut leeks crosswise into 3-inch pieces. *(Bell pepper and leeks can be prepared up to 1 day ahead. Cover separately; refrigerate.)*

Place leeks on platter. Whisk vinegar and mustard in bowl to blend. Gradually whisk in oil. Mix in bell pepper. Season with salt and pepper. Spoon dressing over leeks. Sprinkle cheese, walnuts and mint over leeks. Serve immediately.

4 SERVINGS

Gnocchi with Braised Greens and Wild Mushrooms

◆ ◆ ◆

GNOCCHI

5	ounces soft mild goat cheese (such as Montrachet)
⅓	cup ricotta cheese
⅓	cup all purpose flour
2	egg yolks
1	large egg
¾	teaspoon salt

VEGETABLES

¼	cup olive oil
½	pound fresh wild mushrooms, quartered if large
½	cup finely chopped shallots
8	cups mixed greens (such as spinach and arugula)
2	cups chicken stock or canned low-salt broth
½	cup mixed chopped fresh herbs (such as chives, tarragon, basil and parsley)
3	tablespoons extra-virgin olive oil

FOR GNOCCHI: Mix all ingredients in medium bowl to blend. Cover and refrigerate until cold, about 2 hours.

Line baking sheet with waxed paper. With 2 spoons, shape gnocchi mixture into ovals, using about 1 tablespoon mixture for each; place on prepared sheet. Cook gnocchi in large pot of boiling salted water until tender, about 8 minutes. Using slotted spoon, transfer to clean baking sheet. *(Can be prepared 8 hours ahead. Cover with plastic wrap and refrigerate.)*

FOR VEGETABLES: Heat ¼ cup oil in heavy large skillet over medium heat. Add mushrooms and shallots and sauté 3 minutes. Add greens, stock and herbs and cook until greens wilt, turning occasionally with tongs, about 3 minutes. Season to taste with salt and pepper. Using slotted spoon, divide vegetables among shallow soup bowls. Boil juices left in skillet until slightly thickened, 6 minutes.

Meanwhile, reheat gnocchi in large pot of boiling water until heated through, about 2 minutes.

Using slotted spoon, remove gnocchi from water and arrange atop vegetables. Spoon pan juices over. Drizzle 2 teaspoons olive oil over each serving of gnocchi. Serve immediately.

6 SERVINGS

Crab Salad with Endive and Tomato-Cilantro Sauce

◆ ◆ ◆

CRAB SALAD

2   tablespoons olive oil

2   shallots, thinly sliced

1   teaspoon minced peeled fresh ginger

½   cup chopped tart green apple (such as Granny Smith)

½   cup chopped zucchini

½   cup chopped seeded red bell pepper

½   cup chopped seeded green bell pepper

¼   cup chopped carrot

½   pound crabmeat, drained well, picked over

¼   cup mayonnaise

2   tablespoons chopped fresh chives

SAUCE

2   tomatoes, peeled, seeded, chopped

⅓   cup chopped fresh cilantro

2   tablespoons Sherry wine vinegar

1   garlic clove, chopped
    Pinch of cayenne pepper

½   cup olive oil

2   heads Belgian endive, trimmed, separated into spears
    Chopped fresh chives

FOR CRAB SALAD: Heat oil in heavy large skillet over medium-high heat. Add shallots and ginger and sauté until tender, about 4 minutes. Add apple, zucchini, both bell peppers and carrot and sauté until tender but not brown, 5 minutes. Cool to room temperature.

Mix crabmeat, mayonnaise, 2 tablespoons chopped chives and sautéed vegetables in bowl to blend. Season with salt and pepper. *(Can be prepared 1 day ahead. Cover and refrigerate.)*

FOR SAUCE: Combine tomatoes, cilantro, vinegar, garlic and cayenne in blender and puree until almost smooth. Gradually add oil and blend until thick. Season with salt and pepper.

Arrange endive spears on large platter, tips toward platter edge. Spoon crab salad into center of platter. Drizzle sauce over endive. Garnish salad with chopped fresh chives and serve.

6 SERVINGS

Seafood and Fennel Soup

◆ ◆ ◆

◆ ◆ ◆

A steaming bowlful of this thick soup delivers old-fashioned flavor in less than an hour. Serve with plenty of crusty French bread for a satisfying soup-and-bread supper.

◆ ◆ ◆

1   tablespoon olive oil
8   ounces mushrooms, thickly sliced

6   bacon slices, chopped
1   large onion, coarsely chopped
1   cup thinly sliced fennel
$^1/_4$ cup chopped red bell pepper
1   tablespoon crushed fennel seeds
2   large garlic cloves, chopped
$1^1/_2$ pounds red-skinned potatoes, unpeeled, cut into $^1/_2$-inch pieces
$3^1/_2$ cups canned chicken broth
2   $14^1/_2$-ounce cans diced peeled tomatoes
1   8-ounce can tomato sauce

1   1-pound halibut fillet, cut into 1-inch pieces
8   ounces red snapper fillets, cut into 1-inch pieces
8   ounces sole fillets, cut into 1-inch pieces
    Chopped fresh parsley

Heat oil in heavy large skillet over medium-high heat. Add mushrooms and sauté until golden, about 5 minutes.

Cook bacon in heavy large Dutch oven over medium heat until almost crisp, stirring often, about 3 minutes. Add onion, fennel, bell pepper, fennel seeds and garlic; sauté until vegetables are almost tender, about 5 minutes. Add potatoes, chicken broth, tomatoes with their juices and tomato sauce and bring to boil. Reduce heat and simmer until potatoes are almost tender, about 25 minutes. Mix in mushrooms. *(Can be made 1 day ahead. Cover and refrigerate. Bring soup to simmer before continuing.)*

Add halibut, red snapper and sole to soup and simmer just until fish is cooked through, about 6 minutes. Season with salt and pepper. Ladle into bowls. Sprinkle with parsley.

6 SERVINGS

Spinach Bisque with Sour Cream

◆ ◆ ◆

¼	cup (½ stick) butter
1	large onion, chopped
6	cups canned low-salt chicken broth
1	10-ounce package ready-to-use fresh spinach leaves, large stems removed
2	fresh parsley sprigs
1	large fresh thyme sprig
1	small serrano chili*
2	tablespoons dry Sherry
	Sour cream

Melt butter in heavy large Dutch oven over medium heat. Add onion; sauté until almost tender, about 8 minutes. Add broth, spinach, parsley, thyme and whole chili; bring to boil. Reduce heat; simmer 45 minutes, stirring occasionally.

Discard thyme sprig and chili. Puree soup in blender in batches. Return to same pot. Add Sherry and simmer 5 minutes. Season with salt and pepper. *(Can be made 1 day ahead. Cover; chill. Rewarm before continuing.)* Ladle soup into bowls. Top with dollop of sour cream. Serve immediately.

*A serrano *is a very hot, small fresh green chili available in Latin American markets and many supermarkets.*

4 SERVINGS

Chilled Beet Soup with Dill Cream

◆ ◆ ◆

4 cups (or more) canned low-salt chicken broth
1 pound beets, peeled, chopped
1 cup chopped onion
3/4 cup peeled chopped carrot
2 teaspoons chopped garlic
1 teaspoon sugar

2 tablespoons chopped fresh dill or 2 teaspoons dried dillweed
2 tablespoons chopped fresh chives or green onions
Sour cream

Combine 4 cups broth, beets, onion, carrot and garlic in medium saucepan. Bring to boil. Reduce heat to medium-low; cover and simmer until vegetables are very tender, about 35 minutes. Cool slightly. Puree in blender in batches until smooth. Transfer to bowl. Thin with additional broth if soup is too thick. Mix in sugar. Season with salt and pepper. Cover and chill until cold, at least 4 hours. *(Can be prepared 2 days ahead. Keep refrigerated.)*

Ladle soup into bowls. Sprinkle with dill and chives. Top with sour cream. Serve soup immediately.

4 SERVINGS

◆ ◆ ◆

This pretty and refreshing soup—flavored with curry, cumin, ginger and garlic—is quick to prepare: Just put everything in the blender and puree it. Then chill and serve.

◆ ◆ ◆

Cucumber-Yogurt Soup

◆ ◆ ◆

2 1/4 cups plain yogurt
1 1/4 pounds pickling cucumbers, trimmed, peeled, cut into 1-inch pieces
2 garlic cloves, minced
1 1/2 teaspoons salt
1 1/2 teaspoons ground cumin
1 1/2 teaspoons curry powder
1/4 teaspoon (generous) ground ginger

Thinly sliced radishes

Combine yogurt, cucumbers, garlic, salt, cumin, curry and ginger in blender. Puree until smooth. Strain through fine sieve into large bowl. Refrigerate until well chilled, about 2 hours. *(Can be prepared 1 day ahead. Keep refrigerated.)*

Ladle soup into bowls. Top with radishes and serve.

6 SERVINGS

Carrot Soup with Garden Herbs

◆ ◆ ◆

6   tablespoons olive oil
5   large carrots, thinly sliced
2¹/₂ cups thinly sliced onions
1   teaspoon dried thyme
1   teaspoon golden brown sugar
¹/₂ teaspoon ground nutmeg
4   cups canned chicken broth
¹/₄ cup orange juice
     Chopped fresh chives

Heat olive oil in large saucepan over medium heat. Add carrots and onions and sauté 4 minutes. Add thyme, brown sugar and nutmeg; sauté until vegetables are tender, about 6 minutes. Add chicken broth. Cover pot; simmer until carrots are very soft, about 25 minutes. Using slotted spoon, transfer vegetables to processor. Add ¹/₄ cup cooking liquid. Puree vegetables until smooth. Return puree to pot. Stir in orange juice. Season with salt and pepper. Chill. *(Can be made 1 day ahead. Keep refrigerated.)* Sprinkle with chives.

6 SERVINGS

This lovely chilled soup has a rich, smooth texture even though it contains no cream. It makes a perfect picnic soup. To transport it, bring the cold soup in a thermos and the chives in a plastic bag, and then serve in sturdy ceramic bowls.

◆ ◆ ◆

THE COUNTRY CAPTAIN STORY

Miss Eliza Leslie, in her *New Cookery Book* of 1857, describes "Country Captain" as a curry dish of East Indian origin, having been brought to the States by a British captain of the Sepoys, the native (or "country") troops. While the dish is often associated with Savannah, Georgia, which the captain likely visited on his way home, virtually every other major Southern seaport city also claims Country Captain as its own, suggesting that the mysterious captain made many stops along the coast during his travels on the spice route from India.

Typically, Country Captain is a chicken and curry stew, though the flavors can be incorporated into other kinds of dishes, like the soup here. Early cookbooks called for making homemade curry powder the traditional Indian way, with a distinctive mix of freshly ground spices, including black and red pepper, cloves, cardamon, coriander, cumin and turmeric. These days, the ready-made blends work just fine.

◆ ◆ ◆

Country Captain Soup

◆ ◆ ◆

1	tablespoon olive oil
1	large onion, coarsely chopped
1/2	cup chopped red bell pepper
4	garlic cloves, chopped
6	skinless boneless chicken thighs (about 1 1/4 pounds), cut into 1-inch pieces
1	tablespoon curry powder
1	teaspoon grated peeled fresh ginger
1/4	teaspoon dried crushed red pepper
4	cups (or more) canned chicken broth
2	cups canned diced peeled tomatoes with juices
1	large Granny Smith apple, peeled, coarsely chopped
1/4	cup orzo (rice-shaped pasta; also called riso)
2	tablespoons dried currants
	Chopped fresh cilantro
	Plain yogurt

Heat oil in heavy large Dutch oven over medium-high heat. Add onion, bell pepper and garlic; sauté until vegetables soften, about 5 minutes. Add chicken, curry powder, ginger and crushed red pepper; stir 2 minutes. Add 4 cups broth, tomatoes and apple and bring to boil. Reduce heat and simmer 20 minutes. *(Can be made 1 day ahead. Chill. Bring to simmer before continuing.)*

Stir orzo and currants into soup and simmer until orzo is just cooked through, about 5 minutes. Season with salt and pepper. Ladle soup into bowls. Garnish with cilantro and dollop of yogurt.

6 SERVINGS

Spicy Garbanzo Bean and Turkey Sausage Soup

◆ ◆ ◆

1	teaspoon olive oil
3/4	pound turkey sausage, casings removed, crumbled
8	large garlic cloves, chopped
1	cup canned diced peeled tomatoes with juices
2	tablespoons thinly sliced seeded jalapeño chili
1	teaspoon ground cumin

1   teaspoon chopped fresh rosemary or ¹/₂ teaspoon dried
3   15- to 16-ounce cans garbanzo beans (chick-peas), undrained
2   cups canned chicken broth or beef broth
2   tablespoons fresh lemon juice

    Chopped fresh cilantro
1   avocado, peeled, sliced

Heat olive oil in heavy large Dutch oven over medium-high heat. Add turkey sausage and chopped garlic and sauté until sausage is golden brown and cooked through, breaking up sausage with back of fork, about 5 minutes. Reduce heat to medium. Add tomatoes with their juices, sliced jalapeño chili, ground cumin and chopped fresh rosemary and simmer 10 minutes, stirring frequently. Add garbanzo beans with their liquid and chicken broth and bring to boil. Reduce heat and simmer soup 15 minutes. Stir in fresh lemon juice. Season with salt and pepper. *(Can be prepared 1 day ahead. Cover and refrigerate. Rewarm over medium heat before continuing.)*

Ladle soup into bowls. Sprinkle soup with chopped fresh cilantro and top with sliced avocado. Serve immediately.

6 SERVINGS

◆ ◆ ◆

Sliced or diced fresh avocado makes a colorful garnish for this hearty southwestern soup. If you want to cut up the avocado ahead of time but don't want it to discolor, simply place the avocado pieces in a colander and rinse them with cold water. They will stay bright green for two hours.

◆ ◆ ◆

Crab and Scallop Soup

◆ ◆ ◆

1	1½-pound cooked Dungeness crab
5	quarts water
1	8-ounce bottle clam juice
1	large onion, halved
1	large carrot, peeled
¼	teaspoon dried thyme
¼	teaspoon cayenne pepper
3	tablespoons butter
1	large onion, chopped
3	large garlic cloves, chopped
1½	teaspoons curry powder
½	teaspoon ground turmeric
4	cups peeled 1-inch pieces butternut squash (about 1¾ pounds)
1	10-ounce potato, peeled, cut into 1-inch pieces
1	red bell pepper, cut into ¼-inch strips
1	yellow bell pepper, cut into ¼-inch strips
1	green bell pepper, cut into ¼-inch strips
1½	pounds bay scallops
1½	cups frozen green peas, thawed

Clean crab and crack; remove meat. Reserve shells and crab butter (gray-green coating inside crab shell). Refrigerate crab meat. Place shells and crab butter in 8- to 10-quart stockpot. Add water, clam juice, onion halves, carrot, thyme and cayenne. Boil over medium heat until liquid is reduced to 9 cups, about 1½ hours. Strain.

Melt 2 tablespoons butter in heavy large Dutch oven over medium-high heat. Add chopped onion and garlic and sauté until tender, about 6 minutes. Add curry powder and ground tumeric and stir 1 minute. Add crab stock, butternut squash and potato. Simmer until vegetables are very tender, about 35 minutes. Transfer mixture to blender in batches and puree. Return to Dutch oven. Season with salt and pepper. *(Can be made 1 day ahead; chill.)*

Melt 1 tablespoon butter in large skillet. Add all bell peppers and sauté until crisp-tender, about 2 minutes. Add bay scallops and sauté until almost cooked through, about 3 minutes. Add reserved crab meat and green peas and cook until heated through, about 3 minutes. Season with salt and pepper.

Ladle squash puree into bowls. Top with seafood mixture.

6 SERVINGS

◆ ◆ ◆

This spectacular one-dish meal gets its rich flavor from homemade crab stock. The stock is simple to make and does not require a lot of time. Potato helps thicken the soup; butternut squash adds color.

◆ ◆ ◆

Porcini and White Bean Soup

◆ ◆ ◆

1	ounce dried porcini mushrooms*
2	cups hot water

1	tablespoon olive oil
1	onion, chopped
1³/₄	teaspoons chopped fresh rosemary or ¹/₂ teaspoon dried
2	16-ounce cans cannellini (white kidney beans), rinsed, drained
1	14¹/₂-ounce can vegetable broth
	Additional chopped fresh rosemary

Place mushrooms in medium bowl. Pour 2 cups hot water over; let stand 30 minutes to soften. Remove mushrooms from water, squeezing mushrooms over bowl to remove excess liquid. Chop mushrooms; reserve soaking liquid.

Heat oil in heavy medium saucepan over medium-high heat. Add onion and 1³/₄ teaspoons rosemary and sauté until onion is tender, about 5 minutes. Add mushrooms. Pour in mushroom soaking liquid, leaving any sediment in bottom of bowl. Boil until liquid is very thick, about 8 minutes. Add cannellini and broth; simmer until soup thickens, stirring occasionally, about 10 minutes. Season with salt and pepper. Sprinkle with additional chopped rosemary.

Dried porcini mushrooms are available at Italian markets, specialty foods stores and some supermarkets.

4 SERVINGS

◆ ◆ ◆

Two currently popular ingredients—wild mushrooms and white beans—enhance this richly flavored soup. Low in fat, it's a dish that fits right in with the healthful style of modern American dining.

◆ ◆ ◆

Aromatic Fish Soup with Potatoes

◆ ◆ ◆

4	cups water
1	pound potatoes, peeled, halved lengthwise, cut crosswise into ¹/₂-inch-thick slices
2	medium tomatoes, peeled, quartered
3	garlic cloves, chopped
2	tablespoons chopped fresh mint
1¹/₂	tablespoons fresh lemon juice
1	teaspoon paprika
¹/₂	teaspoon ground cumin
¹/₄	teaspoon dried crushed red pepper

$^1/_3$ cup plus 1 tablespoon finely chopped cilantro or parsley
1 pound 1-inch-thick firm white fish fillets (such as cod or haddock)
3 tablespoons olive oil

Combine first 9 ingredients in large pot. Add $^1/_3$ cup cilantro and bring to boil. Reduce heat, cover and simmer 20 minutes. Uncover and simmer 10 minutes. Add fish and olive oil and simmer until fish is cooked, about 10 minutes. Using back of spoon, break up fish into smaller pieces. Season soup to taste with salt and pepper. Ladle soup into bowls. Sprinkle with 1 tablespoon chopped cilantro and serve immediately.

4 SERVINGS

Vegetable Soup with Pistou

◆ ◆ ◆

PISTOU
$^1/_2$ cup packed fresh basil leaves
$^1/_4$ cup olive oil
$^1/_4$ cup freshly grated Parmesan cheese
2 tablespoons pine nuts

SOUP
5 cups vegetable stock or canned broth
1 small potato (about 5 ounces), peeled, coarsely diced
1 small carrot, peeled, coarsely diced
$^1/_2$ onion, coarsely chopped
$^1/_2$ leek (white and pale green parts only), thinly sliced
1 bay leaf
$1^1/_2$ teaspoons chopped fresh thyme
$^2/_3$ cup drained canned cannellini (white kidney beans)
1 small tomato, peeled, seeded, chopped
1 small zucchini, coarsely diced
2 ounces green beans, trimmed, cut into $^1/_2$-inch lengths

FOR PISTOU: Blend all ingredients in processor to coarse puree. Season with salt and pepper.

FOR SOUP: Bring stock to boil in large saucepan. Add potato, carrot, onion, leek, bay leaf and thyme. Reduce heat; simmer mixture until potato is almost tender, about 10 minutes. Add cannellini, tomato, zucchini and green beans; simmer until green beans are tender, about 4 minutes. Season soup with salt and pepper. Ladle into bowls. Top each with dollop of pistou and serve.

6 SERVINGS

PESTO AND PISTOU

Basil grows in abundance in regions along the Mediterranean, and often finds its way into the local cuisine. One familiar use for the herb is pesto, as it's called in Italy, or *pistou*, as it's known in the south of France. Genoa takes the credit for originating the sauce, which is named for the pestle used to produce this delicious blend of basil, olive oil, garlic, pine nuts and Parmesan and Percorino Romano cheeses.

In this country, we use pesto with Mediterranean abandon—in soups, on pasta, over vegetables or grilled meats and fish. We also like to vary the traditional ingredients, substituting walnuts, pistachios or sunflower seeds, or even different herbs, among them mint, cilantro and rosemary.

Pesto must be made with fresh herbs, which would seemingly make the sauce a seasonal treat. Luckily, pesto keeps beautifully, refrigerated up to four weeks under a thin layer of olive oil in a tightly closed container. Or you can freeze it in tablespoon-size dollops that can be used to add a burst of fresh, summery flavor any time of the year.

◆ ◆ ◆

◆ BEVERAGES ◆

Classic Margaritas

◆ ◆ ◆

Lime wedges
Coarse salt

3½ cups Homemade Sweet and Sour Mix (see recipe below)
1   cup gold tequila
½   cup triple sec
16   ice cubes
12   lime slices

Rub rims of 12 glasses with lime wedges. Dip rims in salt.

Combine 1¾ cups sweet and sour mix, ½ cup tequila, ¼ cup triple sec and 8 ice cubes in blender. Process until well blended. Pour into 6 glasses. Repeat with remaining sweet and sour mix, tequila, triple sec and ice cubes. Pour into 6 glasses. Garnish each with lime.

12 SERVINGS

Homemade Sweet and Sour Mix

3   cups water
3   cups sugar

2   cups fresh lemon juice
2   cups fresh lime juice

Combine water and sugar in large saucepan. Stir syrup over medium heat until sugar dissolves. Bring to boil. Cool syrup.

Mix syrup, lemon juice and lime juice in pitcher. Chill until cold. *(Can be made 1 week ahead. Cover; keep chilled.)*

MAKES 8 CUPS

◆ ◆ ◆

Turn any meal into a party with these refreshing Margaritas. Their secret to success? The do-ahead sweet and sour mix that gets its sweet from a sugar syrup and its sour from fresh lemon and lime juices.

◆ ◆ ◆

Margaritas with Tropical Fruit

❖ ❖ ❖

Lime wedges
Sugar

3 cups Homemade Sweet and Sour Mix (see recipe on page 34)
1 cup gold tequila
12 tablespoons papaya nectar
12 tablespoons guava nectar
½ cup canned cream of coconut*

16 ice cubes
12 lime slices

Rub rims of 12 glasses with lime wedges. Dip rims in sugar.

Combine 1½ cups sweet and sour mix, ½ cup tequila, 6 tablespoons papaya nectar, 6 tablespoons guava nectar, ¼ cup cream of coconut and 8 ice cubes in blender. Process until blended. Pour into 6 glasses. Repeat with remaining sweet and sour mix, tequila, both nectars, cream of coconut and ice cubes. Pour into 6 glasses. Garnish each with lime slice and serve.

Available in the liquor department of most supermarkets.

12 SERVINGS

❖ ❖ ❖

The beef stock makes this robust cocktail a little more bullish than its cousin, the Bloody Mary. In keeping with its demeanor, garnish with green onions rather than celery sticks.

❖ ❖ ❖

Bloody Bull

❖ ❖ ❖

2 cups spicy vegetable juice (such as spicy hot V-8)
 or spicy tomato juice
1 cup canned double-strength beef broth
¾ cup vodka
¼ cup Worcestershire sauce
2 tablespoons fresh lime juice
1 teaspoon garlic powder
4 cups ice cubes
4 green onions, trimmed

Mix vegetable juice, broth, vodka, Worcestershire sauce, lime juice and garlic powder in 4-cup measuring cup. Divide ice cubes among four 12-ounce glasses. Pour juice mixture over and stir to blend. Garnish each with 1 green onion and serve.

4 SERVINGS

Passion's Plaything

◆ ◆ ◆

1   cup sugar
½   cup water

½   cup dark rum
½   cup light rum
½   cup orange juice
½   cup fresh lemon juice
½   cup passion fruit nectar or tropical fruit nectar
½   teaspoon vanilla extract
     Fresh pineapple spears

Stir sugar and water in heavy small saucepan over low heat until sugar dissolves. Increase heat to high and bring to boil. Remove from heat and cool. *(Can be made 4 months ahead. Pour syrup into jar. Cover and refrigerate.)*

Stir both rums, orange juice, lemon juice, passion fruit nectar, vanilla and 6 tablespoons syrup in pitcher. Fill 4 tall glasses with ice. Pour rum mixture over ice. Garnish with pineapple spears.

4 SERVINGS

Mango-Banana Daiquiri

◆ ◆ ◆

1   small banana, peeled
1   9- to 10-ounce mango, peeled, pitted, sliced
½   cup light rum
¼   cup sugar
2   tablespoons fresh lime juice
16   ice cubes

Combine all ingredients in blender and blend until thick and smooth. Pour into stemmed glasses. Serve immediately.

4 SERVINGS

FRUIT DRINKS: A SHORT HISTORY

Long before tropical drinks garnished with pineapple spears and little paper umbrellas became cocktail classics, fruit-based drinks were popular. In colonial America, fruit "bounces" and "shrubs" made with fruit juice and rum or brandy were among the most fashionable forms of liquid refreshment.

Benjamin Franklin's formula for orange shrub entailed a little work, but apparently was well worth the effort. Sugar (two pounds) was dissolved in orange juice (two quarts), then mixed with rum (one gallon). After standing in a wooden cask for three to four weeks, the mixture was carefully filtered ("that not a drop may be lost") and bottled.

Other fruit-based drinks, such as "stone fences" and "sangarees" did not require such a long wait. A stone fence simply paired sweet cider with applejack or bourbon; the mix was served over ice. Named for its blood-red color (from the French *sang*), sangaree combined sliced fruit and red wine with lemon juice, sugar and cinnamon. The drink, which could be made with peaches, strawberries, pineapple or orange, was chilled for an hour and then strained into a glass with sparkling water.

◆ ◆ ◆

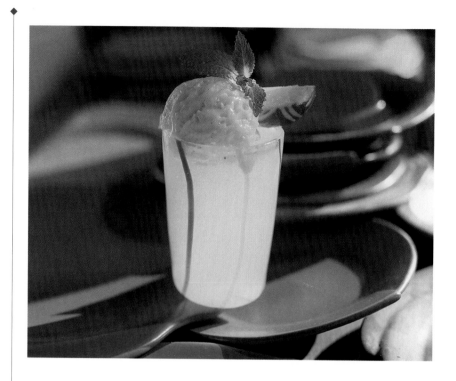

Ice Cream Sodas with Lime, Mint and Ginger

◆ ◆ ◆

1½   cups sugar

1   cup fresh lime juice

¾   cup chopped fresh mint

2   tablespoons chopped fresh ginger

6   cups (about) chilled sparkling water

1½   pints (about) vanilla ice cream or frozen yogurt
     Lime slices (optional)
     Fresh mint sprigs (optional)

Combine sugar, lime juice, chopped mint and ginger in heavy large saucepan. Stir over medium heat until sugar dissolves and syrup comes to simmer. Simmer syrup 2 minutes. Remove from heat and cool completely. Strain syrup into small bowl, pressing lightly on solids; discard solids. *(Can be prepared 1 week ahead. Refrigerate.)*

Pour 3 tablespoons syrup, then ¾ cup sparkling water into each of 6 tall glasses. Stir to blend. Mix in additional syrup or sparkling water to taste. Top each with 1 scoop vanilla ice cream. Garnish sodas with lime slices and mint sprigs, if desired, and serve.

6 SERVINGS

Cranberry-Apple Frappé

◆ ◆ ◆

2   cups chilled cranberry juice cocktail
2   cups chilled apple juice
2   small ripe bananas, peeled, cut into pieces
½   cup sugar
4   tablespoons chilled whipping cream
1   tablespoon fresh lemon juice
8   ice cubes

Combine 1 cup cranberry juice, 1 cup apple juice, 1 banana, ¼ cup sugar, 2 tablespoons cream and ½ tablespoon lemon juice in blender. Process until smooth. Add 4 ice cubes and process until frothy. Divide among 3 glasses. Repeat with remaining ingredients.

6 SERVINGS

Mint Tea

◆ ◆ ◆

4   tea bags of green tea
1   cup packed fresh mint leaves
¼   cup sugar
3   cups boiling water

Place tea bags, fresh mint leaves and sugar in teapot. Pour 3 cups boiling water over mixture and stir to dissolve sugar. Let steep 4 minutes. Serve tea immediately.

6 SERVINGS

This warming drink is a Moroccan specialty. It's usually served in a unique teapot. After the tea brews a bit, some is poured back and forth between the pot and another tea glass, a procedure that is said to improve the brewing process. When ready, the tea is poured from a height of one to two feet into small glasses.

◆ ◆ ◆

◆ Main Courses ◆

Everybody has their favorite main course ingredient, be it beef, chicken, seafood, pork, turkey, lamb, pasta or vegetables. On the following pages, you'll find outstanding recipes that show all of them off to their best advantage.

That there is something here for everyone is practically an understatement when you consider that this selection of the year's best recipes is more varied than even the range of main ingredients would suggest. You'll find, for example, heartwarming dishes such as Braised Veal Shanks with Porcini and Potatoes (page 54) and Turkey Leg Osso Buco (page 88). Showstoppers like Macadamia-crusted Sea Bass with Thai Red Curry Sauce (page 90) and Roast Leg of Lamb with Mustard and Red Wine Sauce (page 56). Quick dishes for after-work suppers, such as Pork and Red Onion Kebabs (page 66), Super-Hot Shrimp Creole (page 105) and Linguine with Clams and Wild Mushrooms (page 126). Healthy meatless entrées, like Rice Pancake with Chunky Tex-Mex Sauce (page 114) and Vegetable Ragout with Cumin and Ginger (page 117).

Just as diverse are the sources of these recipes. Some come from world-class restaurants and chefs and renowned cookbook authors. Others were developed by *Bon Appétit's* own staff experts and frequent contributors. Still others bear the distinctive signatures of our talented readers, who wrote in to share their favorite main courses from their own home kitchens.

Chicken, Ham and Fennel Pot Pies, page 70.

Wine-braised Brisket with Glazed Vegetables

♦ ♦ ♦

♦ ♦ ♦

This impressive dish is deceptively easy to make. The brisket is enhanced with a sauce of white wine and caramelized onions that provides rich flavor, while an assortment of baby vegetables is cooked with thyme and honey for a light complement to the meat. Be sure to start the brisket at least a day before you plan on serving it—although it can be prepared up to three days ahead of time.

♦ ♦ ♦

BRISKET

4 cups canned low-salt chicken broth
1 750-ml bottle dry white wine
½ cup brandy

⅓ cup vegetable oil
2 pounds meaty beef neck bones
3½ pounds onions, thinly sliced
4 large celery stalks, sliced
1½ teaspoons whole allspice
6 garlic cloves, chopped
2 teaspoons dried thyme

1 4½- to 5-pound flat-cut brisket
¾ cup chopped canned tomatoes

1 tablespoon tomato paste

VEGETABLES

2½ pounds mixed baby vegetables (such as zucchini, crookneck and pattypan squashes, turnips, carrots and new potatoes)
8 red boiling onions

¼ cup (½ stick) margarine
¼ cup honey
1 teaspoon dried thyme
10 ounces cherry tomatoes
4 ounces asparagus tips or sugar snap peas

FOR BRISKET: Boil first 3 ingredients in large pot until reduced to 4 cups, approximately 25 minutes.

Preheat oven to 325°F. Heat oil in large Dutch oven over high heat. Add bones; sauté until well browned, turning occasionally, about 12 minutes. Transfer bones to bowl. Add onions, celery and allspice to Dutch oven. Season with salt; cook until onions are golden, stirring often, about 25 minutes. Continue cooking until onions are deep dark brown, scraping bottom of Dutch oven and stirring often, about 15 minutes more. Add garlic and thyme; sauté 5 minutes. Transfer onion mixture to large roasting pan. Add 1 cup broth mixture to Dutch oven. Bring to boil, scraping up browned bits; transfer broth mixture to roasting pan.

Season brisket generously with salt and pepper. Add to Dutch oven and brown over high heat, about 5 minutes per side. Place brisket, fat side up, on onion mixture in roasting pan; surround with bones. Add remaining broth mixture and tomatoes to Dutch oven; bring to boil, scraping up browned bits. Pour mixture over brisket.

Cover roasting pan tightly with heavy-duty foil and place in oven. Bake until brisket is tender, about 3 hours 45 minutes. Remove foil. Cool brisket 2 hours. Refrigerate uncovered 3 hours. Cover brisket tightly and keep chilled 1 day or up to 3 days.

Scrape fat from top of pan juices; discard fat. Transfer brisket to cutting board, scraping gelled juices off brisket back into roasting pan. Bring contents of pan to simmer. Discard bones. Pour contents of roasting pan into coarse strainer set over large bowl. Press on solids to release as much liquid as possible. Puree solids in processor, using on/off turns. Mix enough puree into juices in bowl to form thick sauce. Add tomato paste; whisk to blend. Pour sauce into saucepan and heat through. Season with salt and pepper.

Slice brisket thinly across grain at slight diagonal. Arrange slices in glass baking dish. Drizzle ½ cup sauce over; cover with foil.

FOR VEGETABLES: Bring large pot of salted water to boil. Add all squashes, turnips and carrots and cook until crisp-tender, about 6 minutes. Using slotted spoon, transfer to large bowl. Add potatoes to boiling water and cook until just tender, about 12 minutes. Using slotted spoon, transfer potatoes to same bowl. Add onions to boiling water and cook until almost tender, about 4 minutes. Drain and cool slightly. Peel onions; add to same bowl.

Preheat oven to 350°F. Bake covered brisket until heated through, approximately 30 minutes.

Meanwhile, boil margarine, honey and thyme in heavy large skillet over high heat until syrup is reduced to ⅓ cup, stirring often, about 5 minutes. Add cooked vegetables, tomatoes and asparagus; toss until heated, about 5 minutes. Season with salt and pepper.

Arrange brisket on platter. Bring remaining sauce to simmer. Arrange vegetables around brisket. Serve, passing remaining sauce.

8 TO 10 SERVINGS

◆ ◆ ◆

FAMILY SUPPER FOR EIGHT

WINE-BRAISED BRISKET WITH
GLAZED VEGETABLES
(AT LEFT)

MASHED POTATOES

MIXED GREEN SALAD

COLONIAL BROWN BREAD
(PAGE 164)

DRY RED WINE; MILK

BLUEBERRY SOUR CREAM PIE
(PAGE 172)

◆ ◆ ◆

Lemon and Rosemary T-Bone Steaks

◆ ◆ ◆

1   cup olive oil
⅓   cup fresh lemon juice
⅓   cup chopped fresh rosemary or 1½ tablespoons dried
6   12- to 14-ounce T-bone steaks (each about ¾ to 1 inch thick)

Combine oil, lemon juice, rosemary and generous amount of pepper in large glass baking dish. Add steaks and turn to coat. Cover steaks and refrigerate for 4 to 6 hours.

Prepare barbecue (medium-high heat). Remove steaks from marinade. Sprinkle steaks with salt. Grill to desired doneness, about 4 minutes per side for rare. Transfer to plates and serve.

6 SERVINGS

Roast Beef Salad with Cabbage and Horseradish

◆ ◆ ◆

3   tablespoons prepared white horseradish
2   tablespoons plus 1 teaspoon balsamic vinegar
2¼   teaspoons Dijon mustard
6   tablespoons olive oil

4   cups finely shredded red cabbage

6   ounces thinly sliced roast beef, cut crosswise into strips
1   cup coarsely grated peeled celery root (celeriac)
½   cup thinly sliced red onion
½   cup crumbled Roquefort cheese
     Chopped fresh parsley

Whisk first 3 ingredients in small bowl to blend. Gradually whisk in 5 tablespoons olive oil.

Heat remaining 1 tablespoon oil in large nonstick skillet over medium-high heat. Add cabbage and sauté just until wilted, about 3 minutes. Transfer to large bowl; cool completely.

Mix roast beef, celery root, onion, cheese and dressing into cabbage. Season with salt and pepper. Divide salad between 2 plates. Sprinkle with parsley and serve immediately.

2 SERVINGS

This is heartland food at its best, simplified for today's tastes and pace. In the German communities of middle America, sauerbraten is the Sunday-night meal of choice. Braised red cabbage and egg noodles tossed with butter and poppy seeds are two traditional accompaniments.

◆ ◆ ◆

Skillet Sauerbraten

◆ ◆ ◆

2 tablespoons vegetable oil
8 ounces thinly sliced round steaks
1 large onion, chopped
2 tablespoons crushed gingersnap cookies
¼ teaspoon ground allspice
1 cup canned beef broth
1 to 2 tablespoons red wine vinegar

Heat vegetable oil in heavy large skillet over medium-high heat. Season steaks with salt and pepper. Add steaks to skillet and sear until brown, about 1 minute per side. Transfer steaks to plate. Add chopped onion to skillet. Reduce heat to medium and sauté onion until brown, about 8 minutes. Add crushed gingersnap cookies and ground allspice and stir 1 minute. Add beef broth. Whisk sauce until thick, about 3 minutes. Season with red wine vinegar, salt and pepper. Return steaks and any juices to skillet; simmer 1 minute. Serve sauerbraten immediately.

2 SERVINGS

Grilled T-Bone Steaks with Worcestershire-Chive Butter

◆ ◆ ◆

8 tablespoons (1 stick) butter, room temperature
¼ cup chopped shallots
2 teaspoons minced garlic
3 tablespoons Worcestershire sauce
2 tablespoons dry mustard
2 tablespoons chopped fresh chives

4 10- to 12-ounce T-bone steaks

Melt 1 tablespoon butter in heavy small skillet over medium heat. Add shallots and garlic; sauté until transparent, about 1 minute. Transfer shallot mixture to bowl. Add remaining 7 tablespoons butter, 1 tablespoon Worcestershire sauce, 1 tablespoon dry mustard and 2 tablespoons chives and stir with fork to blend. Season to taste with salt and pepper. Place plastic wrap on work surface. Transfer butter mixture to plastic wrap and form butter into

5-inch-long log. Roll up in plastic, enclosing completely. Refrigerate until firm. *(Can be prepared 3 days ahead. Keep refrigerated.)*

Whisk remaining 2 tablespoons Worcestershire sauce and 1 tablespoon dry mustard in shallow dish. Place steaks in dish and turn to coat. Let stand at room temperature 1 hour.

Prepare barbecue (medium-high heat). Cut butter log into 8 slices. Season steaks with salt and pepper. Grill to desired doneness, about 5 minutes per side for medium-rare. Top each steak with 2 butter slices. Serve immediately.

4 SERVINGS

Rib-Eye Steaks with Port and Mushroom Ragout

◆ ◆ ◆

3	tablespoons butter
5	shallots, sliced
1	pound mixed wild mushrooms, sliced
¾	cup tawny Port
¾	cup canned beef broth
1	tablespoon vegetable oil
4	¾-inch-thick rib-eye steaks (each about 8 ounces), trimmed
¼	cup whipping cream
2	tablespoons chopped fresh tarragon or 2 teaspoons dried Chopped fresh Italian parsley

Melt 2 tablespoons butter in large skillet over medium-high heat. Add sliced shallots and sauté until tender, about 5 minutes. Add mushrooms and stir until beginning to soften, about 6 minutes. Add Port and broth and boil until liquid is syrupy, about 10 minutes.

Melt remaining 1 tablespoon butter with oil in heavy large skillet over high heat. Sprinkle steaks with salt and pepper. Add steaks to skillet and cook to desired doneness, about 3 minutes per side for medium-rare. Transfer steaks to plates.

Bring mushrooms to simmer. Add cream and tarragon and boil until sauce thickens, about 2 minutes. Season with salt and pepper. Spoon mushrooms over steaks. Sprinkle with parsley and serve.

4 SERVINGS

Classic Beef Stew

◆ ◆ ◆

2   pounds well-trimmed boneless beef chuck, cut into 1½-inch pieces
2   cups dry red wine
2   large onions, chopped
1   large carrot, chopped
1   bay leaf
6   fresh thyme sprigs or 1 teaspoon dried
2   garlic cloves, minced

7   bacon slices, cut into ½-inch pieces
    All purpose flour
2   cups beef stock or canned broth
2   large tomatoes, seeded, chopped
4   2 x ½-inch orange peel strips

1½   pounds fettuccine

Combine first 7 ingredients in bowl. Cover and chill overnight. Using tongs, remove beef from marinade and pat dry; reserve marinade. Cook bacon in heavy large Dutch oven over high heat until brown. Using slotted spoon, transfer bacon to paper towels. Season beef with salt and pepper. Toss beef in flour to coat. Working in batches, add beef to drippings in Dutch oven and brown on all sides, about 7 minutes per batch. Return all beef to pot. Add stock, tomatoes, orange peel, marinade and bacon; bring to boil. Reduce heat, cover pan and simmer stew for 1 hour.

Uncover pan and simmer until meat is tender and sauce thickens, stirring occasionally, about 1 hour 15 minutes. Discard bay leaf. Season stew to taste with salt and pepper. *(Can be prepared 1 day ahead. Cover and refrigerate. Bring to simmer before continuing.)*

Cook pasta in large pot of boiling salted water until just tender but still firm to bite, stirring occasionally. Drain. Divide pasta among plates. Top with stew and serve.

6 SERVINGS

◆ ◆ ◆

SUPPER FROM THE SOUTH OF FRANCE FOR SIX

VEGETABLE SOUP WITH PISTOU
(PAGE 33)

CLASSIC BEEF STEW
(AT LEFT; PICTURED OPPOSITE)

FETTUCCINE

RATATOUILLE WITH FRESH BASIL
(PAGE 148)

FRENCH RED WINE

FRESH BERRIES WITH
RASPBERRY LIQUEUR

◆ ◆ ◆

Veal Loin Stuffed with Bell Peppers, Goat Cheese and Basil

◆ ◆ ◆

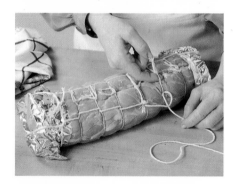

The veal is folded over the filling, then rolled up jelly roll style. Foil on the ends seals the filling, while kitchen string tied around the roll maintains its shape. Bacon slices keep the meat moist during roasting.

◆ ◆ ◆

FILLING

2 large yellow bell peppers
1 3-ounce package cream cheese with chives, room temperature
1 5.3-ounce package basil and roasted garlic goat cheese or
   6 ounces soft fresh goat cheese, room temperature

VEAL

1 4¾-pound center-cut veal rib roast (also known as rack of veal),
   boned, trimmed of all fat and outer membrane
1 bunch fresh arugula, stems trimmed
16 large fresh basil leaves
14 oil-packed sun-dried tomatoes, drained
2 tablespoons (¼ stick) butter
8 bacon slices

SAUCE

2¾ cups canned low-salt chicken broth
3 medium shallots, finely chopped
¼ cup fresh lemon juice
2 tablespoons drained capers
½ cup (1 stick) butter, cut into pieces, room temperature
2 tablespoons chopped fresh Italian parsley

FOR FILLING: Char peppers over gas flame or in broiler until blackened on all sides. Wrap in paper bag; let stand 10 minutes. Peel peppers. Cut lengthwise into quarters; seed and stem peppers. Trim edges of peppers to flatten all sides if necessary. Stir cream cheese and goat cheese in small bowl to blend.

FOR VEAL: Butterfly veal by starting at 1 long side of veal and cutting horizontally to within 1 inch of opposite long side. Open veal as for book. Place large sheet of plastic wrap over cut surface of veal. Using meat pounder or rolling pin, pound veal to generous ½-inch even thickness, forming rectangle approximately 10 x 12 inches. Season veal with salt and pepper.

Blanch arugula in saucepan of boiling water just until wilted, about 2 seconds. Drain; rinse with cold water. Drain well on paper towels; pat dry. Repeat blanching process with basil leaves. Overlap arugula leaves down center of veal, forming 2-inch-wide by 12-inch-long strip. Cover with half of roasted bell peppers, skinned side down. Top with drained sun-dried tomatoes, arranged in 2 rows.

Set aside ¼ cup cheese mixture for sauce. Spoon remaining cheese mixture in even log atop sun-dried tomatoes. Arrange remaining bell peppers, skinned side up, over cheese mixture. Arrange blanched basil leaves over bell peppers.

Fold 1 long side of veal over filling. Tightly roll up veal jelly roll style. Cover ends of veal roll with heavy-duty aluminum foil to enclose filling completely. Tie kitchen string around veal roll every 1½ inches to maintain neat log shape. Wrap string lengthwise around veal roll to secure foil at ends, weaving string alternately under and over crosswise ties. Cover veal and cheese mixture separately; refrigerate until well chilled, at least 6 hours and up to 1 day.

Preheat oven to 375°F. Melt butter in heavy large shallow roasting pan over medium-high heat. Season veal with salt and pepper. Place veal in pan and brown on all sides, turning frequently, about 10 minutes. Remove pan from heat; cool veal 15 minutes. Drape bacon slices over veal, tucking ends under veal.

Roast veal until thermometer inserted into center of meat (not filling) registers 140°F, about 45 minutes. Transfer to work surface. Let veal stand for 15 minutes.

FOR SAUCE: Combine broth and shallots in heavy medium saucepan. Boil over high heat until mixture is reduced to ½ cup, about 20 minutes. Whisk in lemon juice and capers. Reduce heat to low; gradually whisk in butter, then reserved ¼ cup cheese mixture and parsley. Season sauce to taste with salt and pepper.

To serve, remove bacon, string and foil. Cut veal crosswise into even slices. Spoon some sauce onto each plate. Top with 2 slices.

8 SERVINGS

◆ ◆ ◆

This stylish dinner party dish comes with a bonus: Much of the prep work can be done a day ahead of time. At the store, have the butcher bone and trim all of the fat and membrane from a 4¾-pound center-cut veal rib roast, resulting in a 3-pound oblong boneless veal loin.

◆ ◆ ◆

Osso Buco with Gremolata

◆ ◆ ◆

VEAL

¼   cup (½ stick) butter

6   tablespoons olive oil

2   cups chopped onions

1   cup chopped carrots

1   cup chopped celery

4   large garlic cloves, chopped

12   center-cut pieces veal shank (each 1½ inches thick)
      All purpose flour

1   cup dry white wine

4   cups canned beef broth

1¾   cups chopped canned Italian-style tomatoes with juices

2   bay leaves

2   3-inch-long strips lemon peel (yellow part only)

1   teaspoon dried thyme

1   teaspoon dried basil

⅛   teaspoon ground nutmeg

GREMOLATA

½   cup chopped Italian parsley

2   tablespoons grated lemon peel

4   large garlic cloves, minced

◆ ◆ ◆

Gremolata—a mixture of chopped Italian parsley, grated lemon peel and minced garlic—accents this traditional and delicious Italian veal dish.

◆ ◆ ◆

FOR VEAL: Melt butter with 2 tablespoons olive oil in heavy large Dutch oven over medium-high heat. Add onions, carrots, celery and garlic and sauté until vegetables are tender and golden brown, about 15 minutes. Remove Dutch oven from heat.

Season veal with salt and pepper. Coat with flour; shake off excess. Heat 4 tablespoons oil in heavy large skillet over high heat. Working in batches, add veal to skillet and brown on all sides, about 8 minutes per batch. Arrange veal on vegetables in Dutch oven.

Pour off fat from skillet. Add wine and boil 3 minutes, scraping up any browned bits. Pour wine mixture over veal. Add broth, tomatoes with their juices, bay leaves, lemon peel, thyme, basil and nutmeg to Dutch oven. Bring to boil. Reduce heat; cover and simmer until veal is very tender, about 1 hour 40 minutes. (*Can be prepared 1 day ahead. Refrigerate uncovered until cold. Cover and keep refrigerated. Bring to simmer over medium heat before continuing.*)

FOR GREMOLATA: Mix parsley, lemon peel and garlic in bowl.

Mix half of gremolata into veal; simmer 5 minutes to blend flavors. Using tongs, transfer veal to platter; tent with foil to keep warm. Boil cooking liquid until reduced to 3 cups, about 15 minutes. Season sauce to taste with salt and pepper. Pour sauce over veal. Sprinkle with remaining gremolata.

12 SERVINGS

Veal with Vinegar Sauce

◆ ◆ ◆

⅓   cup all purpose flour
     Pinch of cayenne pepper
1   pound veal (preferably top round), cut into ¼-inch-thick slices
3   tablespoons olive oil

4   garlic cloves, minced
¼   cup red wine vinegar
1½   cups canned unsalted beef broth
½   cup packed chopped fresh Italian parsley

Stir flour and pinch of cayenne pepper in shallow pie dish. Lightly coat veal with flour mixture, shaking off excess. Heat olive oil in large nonstick skillet over medium-high heat. Add veal in batches and cook just until outside is no longer pink, about 1 minute per side. Transfer veal to platter. Set aside.

Add minced garlic to skillet and sauté 1 minute. Return veal to skillet. Pour vinegar over (mixture will steam). Pour beef broth over. Boil until sauce is reduced by half and veal is tender, about 6 minutes. Transfer veal to platter. Tent with aluminum foil to keep warm. Add chopped parsley to skillet. Cook until sauce is thick, about 5 minutes. Season to taste with salt. Pour over veal and serve.

4 SERVINGS

Braised Veal Shanks with Porcini and Potatoes

◆ ◆ ◆

1	ounce dried porcini mushrooms
2	cups hot water
4	tablespoons olive oil
2	large onions, chopped
2	garlic cloves, chopped
2	teaspoons dried rosemary
2	bay leaves
1	pound button mushrooms, sliced
3	large red-skinned potatoes, cut into ½-inch-thick slices
6	1-inch-thick veal shanks
	All purpose flour
1	cup dry white wine
1½	cups canned beef broth
2	tablespoons fresh lemon juice
1	10-ounce package frozen peas, thawed
3	tablespoons chopped fresh parsley
1	tablespoon chopped lemon peel

Place porcini in bowl. Pour water over; let stand until soft, about 30 minutes. Drain, reserving liquid. Chop porcini.

Preheat oven to 350°F. Heat 2 tablespoons oil in heavy large Dutch oven over medium-high heat. Add onions, garlic, rosemary and bay leaves; sauté until tender, about 10 minutes. Add fresh and dried mushrooms and potatoes; cook 4 minutes, stirring often.

Heat 2 tablespoons oil in heavy large skillet over high heat. Season veal with salt and pepper. Coat with flour. Add to skillet; brown well, about 4 minutes per side. Place atop vegetables in Dutch oven. Add wine to skillet; bring to boil, stirring up any browned bits. Boil until liquid is reduced by half, about 3 minutes. Add to Dutch oven. Add porcini soaking liquid, leaving any sediment behind. Add broth and juice. Bring to boil. Cover, place in oven and bake until tender, 1 hour 15 minutes. *(Can be made 1 day ahead; chill.)*

Uncover stew; cook over medium-high heat until liquid is thickened, stirring occasionally, 15 minutes. Season with salt and pepper. Discard bay leaves. Add peas; heat through.

Mix parsley and lemon peel. Top stew with parsley mixture.

4 SERVINGS

Grilled Veal Chops with Merlot Sauce

◆ ◆ ◆

3   tablespoons olive oil

1½   cups chopped carrots

1½   cups chopped celery

1½   cups chopped onions

3   tablespoons tomato paste

3   tablespoons whole black peppercorns

1½   tablespoons chopped fresh rosemary or 1½ teaspoons dried

1   tablespoon grated lemon peel

2   bay leaves

1   750-ml bottle Merlot or other dry red wine

1½   cups beef stock or canned broth

1½   cups chicken stock or canned low-salt broth

4   10-ounce veal chops (about 1 inch thick)

Heat oil in heavy large skillet over high heat. Add carrots, celery and onions; sauté until vegetables are brown, about 10 minutes. Add tomato paste; stir 30 seconds. Add peppercorns, chopped rosemary, lemon peel and bay leaves; stir 1 minute. Add wine. Boil until mixture is thick, about 15 minutes. Add both stocks and bring to boil. Reduce heat and simmer until liquid is reduced to about ¾ cup and thickens to sauce consistency, about 20 minutes. Strain sauce. Season with salt and pepper. *(Can be made 1 day ahead. Cover and refrigerate. Bring to simmer before using.)*

Prepare barbecue (medium-high heat) or preheat broiler. Season veal with salt and pepper. Grill or broil to desired doneness, about 5 minutes per side for medium-rare. Transfer veal to plates. Spoon sauce over and then serve immediately.

4 SERVINGS

WILDER WILD MUSHROOMS

Wild mushrooms are not the exotic ingredient they used to be. They are a regular on restaurant menus across the country, and most of the bigger supermarkets now keep several of them in stock for home cooks. Chanterelles, porcini and morels...these are some of the wild mushrooms we know and love.

But these, in fact, are just the tip of the mushroom iceberg. There are thousands of different kinds, both cultivated and wild, growing around the world. Here are some of the less familiar varieties to watch out for.

◆ Fairy Ring: So named for the small brown rings on their stems, these unusual wild mushrooms have a delicate flavor that works well with poultry, seafood and in soups.

◆ Hen-of-the-Woods: Long, slow cooking is necessary to bring out the tender texture and rich flavor of these ruffled, spoon-shaped, grayish-brown fungi.

◆ Portobello: Large and taupe or brown in color, these meaty mushrooms can be grilled or roasted.

◆ Trompettes-des-Morts: Also known as Horns of Plenty, these thin, black, trumpet-shaped mushrooms have a nutty flavor that goes well with pork and poultry dishes.

◆ ◆ ◆

Roast Leg of Lamb with Mustard and Red Wine Sauce

♦ ♦ ♦

1   6- to 6¼-pound leg of lamb, large bone removed,
    shank bone left intact
5   large garlic cloves, pressed
2   tablespoons mustard seeds
1   tablespoon dry mustard
1   tablespoon Dijon mustard
1   teaspoon salt
1   teaspoon ground pepper

1   750-ml bottle Cabernet Sauvignon or other dry red wine
3   cups unsalted beef stock or canned unsalted broth
1   14½-ounce can low-salt chicken broth
3   large shallots, finely chopped

Additional dry mustard
Fresh parsley sprigs

Trim all fat and connective tissue from lamb. Stir garlic, mustard seeds, 1 tablespoon dry mustard, Dijon mustard, salt and pepper in bowl to form paste. Spread half of paste over 1 side of lamb. Place piece of plastic wrap large enough to cover lamb in baking dish. Place lamb atop plastic wrap, paste side down. Spread remaining paste over second side of lamb. Gather plastic around lamb, covering completely. Chill overnight.

Combine wine, beef stock, chicken broth and shallots in large saucepan. Boil until liquid is reduced to generous 1 cup, about 45 minutes. *(Sauce can be made 1 day ahead. Cover and chill.)*

Preheat oven to 375°F. Remove plastic from lamb. Place lamb on rack in roasting pan. Sprinkle with additional dry mustard, salt and pepper. Roast until thermometer inserted into thickest part of lamb registers 125°F, about 1 hour 30 minutes. Place on platter. Add sauce to pan. Bring to boil, scraping up any browned bits. Garnish lamb with parsley; carve at the table. Pass sauce separately.

6 SERVINGS

ABOUT TAGINES

Named for the shallow earthen-ware dish with a conical lid in which they are traditionally oven-simmered and then served, *tagines* are the richly flavored stews of Morocco. Traditionally, housewives would take their tagine to the local bakery, where it would cook in the huge oven all day. The result would be meltingly tender meat and vegetables in a rich and highly seasoned sauce.

The variety of tagines is enormous. Often, less-expensive cuts of beef and lamb are cooked in this way, though you'll find chicken, fish and vegetable tagines, too. The unique flair with which Moroccan cooking combines spices ensures that any tagine, whatever its main ingredients, will be intensely flavored. Tagines can be made spicy with garlic and chilies or fragrant with cinnamon and almonds, sweet with raisins and onions or tangy with saffron and olives. Fish tagines are usually prepared with a marinade called *charmoula*, made from paprika, cumin, cilantro and garlic. Couscous is the classic accompaniment to tagines of all kinds.

◆ ◆ ◆

Lamb Tagine with Almonds

◆ ◆ ◆

½ cup (1 stick) butter
3 pounds boneless lamb shoulder or stew meat, cut into 1½-inch pieces
2 cups chopped onion
1½ cups water
¼ teaspoon saffron threads
1 cinnamon stick

¾ pound pitted prunes
3 tablespoons honey
2¼ teaspoons ground cinnamon

1 cup blanched slivered almonds, toasted
1 tablespoon sesame seeds, toasted

Melt ¼ cup butter in heavy large Dutch oven over high heat. Season lamb with salt and pepper. Working in batches, add to pot and sauté until brown on all sides, about 3 minutes per batch. Using slotted spoon, transfer lamb to bowl. Add onion to pot; sauté 2 minutes. Return lamb to pot. Stir in water, saffron, cinnamon stick and ¼ cup butter. Bring to boil. Reduce heat, cover and simmer until meat is tender, stirring occasionally, about 1 hour 30 minutes.

Using slotted spoon, transfer lamb to large bowl. Discard cinnamon stick. Add pitted prunes to pot and simmer 10 minutes. Stir in 3 tablespoons honey and ground cinnamon. Increase heat and boil until mixture resembles thick syrup, stirring frequently, about 15 minutes. Return lamb to Dutch oven. Season lamb mixture to taste with salt and pepper. *(Can be prepared 1 day ahead. Refrigerate.)*

Cook lamb mixture over low heat until heated through. Spoon onto serving platter. Sprinkle with almonds and sesame.

6 SERVINGS

Grilled Ground Lamb Kebabs with Fresh Hot-Pepper Paste

◆ ◆ ◆

1¼ pounds ground lamb
¾ cup finely chopped onion
½ cup finely chopped fresh parsley

½   cup finely chopped fresh cilantro

4   garlic cloves, minced

¾   teaspoon salt

½   teaspoon ground black pepper

½   teaspoon paprika

½   teaspoon cayenne pepper

12 bamboo skewers

Olive oil

Warm pita bread

Fresh Hot-Pepper Paste (see recipe below)

Combine lamb, onion, parsley, cilantro, garlic, salt, pepper, paprika and cayenne in large bowl and mix well. *(Can be prepared 6 hours ahead. Cover and refrigerate.)* Place bamboo skewers in shallow dish. Cover with cold water and let stand at least 1 hour.

Prepare barbecue (medium-high heat). Drain skewers. Form generous ¼ cup lamb mixture into 3-inch-long sausage around center of 1 bamboo skewer. Repeat with remaining lamb mixture and skewers. Brush lamb kebabs with oil. Grill kebabs until brown and cooked through, turning frequently, about 12 minutes. Serve in warm pita bread with Fresh Hot-Pepper Paste.

MAKES 12 KEBABS

Fresh Hot-Pepper Paste

1   cup chopped fresh cilantro

1   cup chopped fresh parsley

¼   cup chopped seeded fresh red serrano or red jalapeño chilies

¼   cup water

¼   cup olive oil

1½   tablespoons minced garlic

1   teaspoon salt

1   teaspoon ground black pepper

1   teaspoon ground cumin

Combine all ingredients in processor and blend until very finely chopped. *(Can be prepared 1 week ahead. Refrigerate.)*

MAKES ABOUT 1 CUP

◆ ◆ ◆

This is a typical Israeli dish, where kebabs of spiced ground lamb are usually served with pita and various condiments, one of which is a hot-pepper relish. There are many different kinds of these relishes—the Fresh Hot-Pepper Paste here is an easy one.

◆ ◆ ◆

Grilled Rosemary Lamb Chops

♦ ♦ ♦

¾   cup balsamic vinegar
6   tablespoons olive oil
3   tablespoons fresh lemon juice
3   tablespoons minced fresh rosemary or 3 teaspoons dried
6   garlic cloves, minced
1   teaspoon ground black pepper
12   1-inch-thick loin lamb chops, fat trimmed

Mix first 6 ingredients in small bowl. Place lamb chops in single layer in 13 x 9 x 2-inch glass dish. Pour marinade over. Cover and refrigerate 4 hours, turning chops occasionally.

Prepare barbecue (medium-high heat). Season lamb with salt and pepper and place on grill. Cover; grill chops to desired doneness, basting with marinade, about 4 minutes per side for medium-rare.

4 SERVINGS

Lamb Chops with Nut Crust

♦ ♦ ♦

½   cup blanched slivered almonds (about 2¼ ounces)
½   cup pine nuts (about 2½ ounces)
½   cup pistachios (about 2½ ounces)
½   cup walnuts (about 2¼ ounces)
½   cup seasoned Italian-style dry breadcrumbs
1   cup all purpose flour
2   large eggs
1   teaspoon milk
8   1- to 1½-inch-thick loin lamb chops (each about 4 ounces)
2   tablespoons olive oil

Preheat oven to 425°F. Grind all nuts in processor until finely chopped. Transfer to medium bowl; add breadcrumbs. Season with salt and pepper. Place flour in another medium bowl. Whisk eggs and milk in another bowl to blend. Coat lamb chops with flour. Dip into egg mixture, then nut mixture, coating completely.

Heat 2 tablespoons oil in heavy large skillet over medium heat. Add lamb chops to skillet in batches and cook until golden brown, about 2 minutes per side. Transfer to baking sheet. Bake chops to desired doneness, about 12 minutes for medium-rare.

4 SERVINGS

♦ ♦ ♦

PROVENÇAL DINNER FOR FOUR

GRILLED ROSEMARY LAMB CHOPS
(AT LEFT; PICTURED OPPOSITE)

TWO-BEAN AND ROASTED
RED PEPPER SALAD
(PAGE 161; PICTURED OPPOSITE)

GRILLED TOMATOES WITH AIOLI
(PAGE 143; PICTURED OPPOSITE)

BREADSTICKS

LIGHTLY CHILLED RED BANDOL
OR BEAUJOLAIS

FRESH RASPBERRIES AND CREAM

CRISP BUTTER COOKIES

♦ ♦ ♦

Lamb Moussaka with Currants

◆ ◆ ◆

◆ ◆ ◆

This eggplant and lamb casserole is known the world over as the Greek national dish. In this lightened version, it's topped with yogurt rather than the customary béchamel sauce.

◆ ◆ ◆

5	tablespoons olive oil
3	large green bell peppers, seeded, cut into ½-inch pieces
1½	pounds ground lamb
2	cups chopped onion
⅔	cup dry red wine
1	teaspoon cayenne pepper
2	28-ounce cans Italian-style tomatoes, drained, chopped
½	cup dried currants
2	tablespoons tomato paste
	Pinch of ground nutmeg
2	large eggplants (about 2¼ pounds total), cut lengthwise into ¼-inch-thick slices
2	teaspoons sea salt
	Olive oil
1	pound russet potatoes (about 2 medium), peeled
3	cups plain yogurt (do not use low-fat or nonfat)
3	large egg yolks

Heat 2 tablespoons olive oil in heavy large Dutch oven over medium-high heat. Add peppers and sauté until tender and beginning to color, about 8 minutes. Transfer peppers to bowl. Heat remaining 3 tablespoons oil in same Dutch oven over medium-high heat. Add lamb and sauté until cooked through, breaking up with back of spoon, about 6 minutes. Add onion and sauté until onion is tender, about 6 minutes. Add wine and cayenne pepper and cook 2 minutes. Stir in tomatoes, currants, tomato paste and nutmeg. Reduce heat to medium. Cover and simmer until sauce is very thick and reduced to 6 cups, stirring occasionally, about 1 hour 10 minutes. Season to taste with salt and pepper.

Meanwhile, line large baking sheet with foil. Arrange eggplant slices in layers on prepared sheet, sprinkling each layer with sea salt. Let stand at room temperature 30 minutes.

Preheat broiler. Line another large baking sheet with foil. Pat eggplant slices dry with paper towels. Arrange some of eggplant slices in single layer on second prepared sheet. Brush lightly with olive oil

on both sides. Broil until golden brown, about 4 minutes per side. Transfer to platter. Repeat with remaining eggplant.

Boil potatoes in large pot of salted water 5 minutes. Drain. Cool. Cut potatoes into ¼-inch-thick slices.

Preheat oven to 400°F. Coat 13 x 9 x 2-inch glass baking dish with oil. Arrange potatoes in bottom of dish. Arrange half of eggplant slices over potatoes. Pour half of sauce over. Arrange sautéed peppers over sauce. Arrange remaining eggplant slices over peppers. Pour remaining sauce over eggplant.

Bake moussaka until bubbling around edges, about 45 minutes. Spoon off any excess fat. Using back of spoon, press down on moussaka to compact layers. Whisk yogurt and egg yolks in medium bowl to blend. Pour over moussaka, covering completely. Bake until yogurt topping is softly set, about 15 minutes. Transfer baking dish to rack and let stand 20 minutes. *(Can be prepared 1 day ahead. Cool. Cover and refrigerate. Rewarm in 400°F oven until heated through, about 30 minutes.)* Spoon moussaka onto plates.

8 SERVINGS

Pork Chops with Caramelized Onions and Smoked Gouda

◆ ◆ ◆

6   tablespoons vegetable oil

8   1-inch-thick center-cut rib pork chops (each about 8 ounces)

1   cup plus 5 tablespoons all purpose flour

1   teaspoon plus 1 tablespoon Hungarian sweet paprika

8   cups sliced onions (about 4 large)

1   teaspoon sugar

4   teaspoons minced garlic

4   cups (about) canned beef broth

¾   cup grated smoked Gouda cheese with rind (about 3 ounces)

3   tablespoons butter

Preheat oven to 350°F. Heat 3 tablespoons oil in heavy large skillet over high heat. Season pork with salt and pepper. Dredge in 1 cup flour; shake off excess. Working in batches, add pork to skillet and sauté until brown, about 3 minutes per side. Arrange pork in single layer in 15 x 10 x 2-inch glass baking dish. Sprinkle 1 teaspoon paprika over pork. Set aside.

Discard contents of skillet; wipe clean. Add 3 tablespoons oil; heat over medium-high heat. Add onions; sprinkle with sugar and sauté until well browned, stirring often, about 20 minutes. Add garlic; sauté 1 minute. Add 1 tablespoon paprika. Place onions over pork. Pour enough broth over so that chops are almost covered. Cover with foil. Bake until pork is tender, about 45 minutes.

Reduce oven temperature to 200°F. Using tongs, transfer pork to large bowl, leaving onion mixture in baking dish. Pour contents of baking dish into strainer set over medium bowl. Return onion mixture to same baking dish, spreading evenly (reserve cooking liquid). Arrange pork atop onions; sprinkle with cheese. Cover dish with foil; transfer dish to oven to keep warm.

Melt butter in heavy large saucepan over medium heat. Add 5 tablespoons flour. Cook until mixture just begins to color, whisking often (mixture will be dry and crumbly), about 4 minutes. Gradually whisk in reserved cooking liquid. Bring sauce to boil, whisking constantly. Boil until thickened, whisking often, about 5 minutes. Season with salt and pepper. Transfer pork and onions to plates. Spoon sauce around pork and serve.

8 SERVINGS

◆ ◆ ◆

SUNDAY NIGHT SUPPER FOR EIGHT

CRUDITÉS AND DIP

PORK CHOPS WITH CARAMELIZED ONIONS AND SMOKED GOUDA
(AT RIGHT; PICTURED OPPOSITE)

EGG NOODLES WITH CARAWAY

SAUTÉED CARROTS

CABERNET SAUVIGNON

BAKED PEARS WITH HONEY AND GINGER
(PAGE 182)

◆ ◆ ◆

Pork and Red Onion Kebabs

◆ ◆ ◆

1½   pounds pork tenderloin, cut into 16 equal pieces
1   red onion, cut into 16 equal pieces
8   8- to 10-inch bamboo skewers, soaked in water 10 minutes

⅓   cup vegetable oil
¼   cup dry red wine
3   tablespoons red wine vinegar
3   tablespoons soy sauce
1   tablespoon chopped garlic
1   tablespoon chopped peeled fresh ginger
1½   teaspoons sugar

Thread 2 pieces of pork and 2 pieces of onion alternately on each skewer. Season with salt and pepper. Arrange kebabs in 13 x 9 x 2-inch glass baking dish.

Whisk all remaining ingredients in medium bowl. Pour marinade over kebabs. Let stand up to 2 hours at room temperature or cover and refrigerate up to 1 day, turning occasionally.

Preheat broiler. Drain marinade into small saucepan. Boil marinade 2 minutes. Broil kebabs until pork is cooked through, turning frequently and basting with marinade, about 12 minutes.

4 SERVINGS

Pork Tenderloin with Sautéed Onion and Fennel and Fennel Cream

◆ ◆ ◆

3   tablespoons olive oil
2   teaspoons fennel seeds, crushed
2   medium fennel bulbs, quartered, cored, thinly sliced
1   large onion, thinly sliced
2   tablespoons minced garlic

2   12-ounce pork tenderloins, trimmed, each cut crosswise in half

3   large shallots, minced
½   cup dry white wine
1½   cups canned low-salt chicken broth
½   cup whipping cream

Heat 2 tablespoons olive oil in heavy large skillet over medium-high heat. Add 1 teaspoon crushed fennel seeds and stir until fragrant, about 30 seconds. Reduce heat to meduim-low. Stir in sliced fennel and onion and sauté until vegetables are very tender and caramelized, about 40 minutes. Add 1 tablespoon minced garlic and sauté until tender, about 5 minutes. Season with salt and pepper. *(Mixture can be prepared 1 day ahead. Cover and refrigerate.)*

Preheat oven to 450°F. Heat 1 tablespoon olive oil in another heavy large skillet over high heat. Season pork tenderloins with salt and pepper. Add pork to skillet; cook until brown on all sides, about 10 minutes. Transfer pork to baking sheet; reserve drippings in skillet. Roast pork until thermometer inserted into center registers 150°F, about 5 minutes. Remove from oven; keep warm.

Meanwhile, add minced shallots and remaining 1 teaspoon crushed fennel seeds and 1 tablespoon garlic to skillet with drippings and sauté over medium heat until shallots are tender, about 2 minutes. Increase heat to high. Add white wine and boil until liquid is reduced to glaze, about 2 minutes. Add chicken broth and whipping cream and boil until reduced to sauce consistency, whisking often, about 5 minutes. Season sauce to taste with salt and pepper.

Rewarm fennel mixture over medium heat until heated through. Divide fennel mixture among 4 plates. Cut pork into ½-inch-thick rounds. Arrange pork atop fennel. Spoon sauce over pork.

4 SERVINGS

♦ ♦ ♦

ELEGANT DINNER FOR FOUR

SMOKED TROUT ON TOASTS

PORK TENDERLOIN WITH
SAUTÉED ONION AND FENNEL
AND FENNEL CREAM
(AT LEFT; PICTURED AT LEFT)

POTATO AND CELERY ROOT PUREE
(PAGE 150; PICTURED AT LEFT)

STEAMED BROCCOLI

ZINFANDEL

CHOCOLATE-HAZELNUT MOUSSE
(PAGE 200)

COFFEE

♦ ♦ ♦

Chili-baked Ribs

♦ ♦ ♦

SAUCE

4	teaspoons olive oil
1	cup minced onion
1½	cups water
1	cup ketchup
⅔	cup packed golden brown sugar
⅔	cup cider vinegar
¼	cup unsulfured (light) molasses
2	tablespoons Worcestershire sauce
2	tablespoons instant coffee powder
2	teaspoons prepared mustard
2	teaspoons chili powder
1	teaspoon ground cumin
¼	teaspoon ground cinnamon
¼	teaspoon cayenne pepper

RIBS

6	baby back pork rib racks (about 9 pounds total weight)
½	cup cider vinegar
4	teaspoons liquid smoke flavoring
6	tablespoons chili powder
3	tablespoons ground cumin
1	tablespoon golden brown sugar
1½	teaspoons onion powder
¼	teaspoon cayenne pepper

♦ ♦ ♦

SOUTHWESTERN SUPPER FOR EIGHT

CHILI-BAKED RIBS
(AT RIGHT; PICTURED AT RIGHT)

PINTO BEANS WITH
TORTILLA-CHEESE CRUST
(PAGE 144; PICTURED AT RIGHT)

AVOCADO, CITRUS AND
RED ONION SALAD

BEER

MARGARITA CHEESECAKE
(PAGE 193)

♦ ♦ ♦

FOR SAUCE: Heat oil in heavy large saucepan over medium heat. Add onion and sauté until translucent, about 5 minutes. Whisk in remaining ingredients. Bring to boil. Reduce heat; simmer until reduced to 3 cups, stirring occasionally, about 30 minutes. *(Can be prepared 1 week ahead. Cover and refrigerate.)*

FOR RIBS: Score white membrane on underside of ribs. Place ribs in large roasting pan. Mix vinegar and liquid smoke in small bowl; brush over both sides of ribs. Refrigerate 2 hours.

Preheat oven to 350°F. Mix chili powder, cumin, sugar, onion powder and cayenne. Rub over both sides of ribs. Season with salt and pepper. Arrange ribs, meat side up, in single layer on 2 baking sheets. Roast 1¾ hours, covering with foil if browning too quickly.

Remove ribs from oven. Brush both sides of ribs with ¾ cup sauce. Roast 10 minutes. Brush both sides of ribs with additional ¾ cup sauce. Roast 15 minutes longer. Remove ribs from oven. Cover with foil; let ribs stand for 15 minutes.

Cut ribs between bones into 3- to 4-rib sections. Serve ribs immediately with remaining sauce.

8 SERVINGS

"Drunken" Pork Chops

◆ ◆ ◆

4	½-inch-thick center-cut pork chops
1	tablespoon olive oil
1	onion, chopped
1½	teaspoons fennel seeds
2	teaspoons paprika
½	cup dry white wine
½	cup canned low-salt chicken broth
1	teaspoon fresh lemon juice

Season pork with salt and pepper. Heat oil in heavy large skillet over medium-high heat. Add pork; sauté until brown and just cooked through, about 5 minutes per side. Transfer pork to plate; tent with foil to keep warm. Add onion and fennel seeds to same skillet and sauté until onion is tender, about 5 minutes. Mix in paprika; stir 15 seconds. Add wine, broth and lemon juice and boil until sauce thickens slightly, scraping up browned bits, about 5 minutes. Season sauce with salt and pepper. Spoon sauce over pork chops.

4 SERVINGS

RIB BASICS

Alongside the bone lie some of the tastiest portions of meat. In beef, the tenderest steaks and roasts come from the rib section near the loin: rib eye, Delmonico, rib roasts. Meaty short ribs are good for slow braising or stewing. And beef back ribs make excellent barbecue fare.

The very best ribs for barbecuing, though, come from pork. The meatiest ribs are country-style, cut from the blade end of the loin. Baby back ribs, cut from the loin, are slightly less meaty but tender and flavorful; they're generally sold in racks. The all-around favorite, spareribs, come from the breast and lower rib cage and have little meat but lots of flavor.

Whatever cut you choose, if you're going to barbecue, it's a good idea to first cook the ribs slowly in the oven for 30 to 40 minutes. This helps to reduce the amount of fat. Then grill them in a closed barbecue over a medium-hot fire for 10 to 15 minutes per side, generously brushing with your favorite barbecue sauce.

◆ ◆ ◆

Baking meats under a pastry crust is a culinary tradition as ancient as the Greeks. In medieval Europe, many an elegant banquet ended with the presentation of a fanciful pastry creation that held a stew of beef, game, raisins and spices—or even live birds that fluttered out when the pie was cut open to serve.

During medieval times, the pot pie became especially popular in England, where it has remained a favorite to this day. It was used then, as it often is now, to stretch ingredients, with leftovers—like a few bites of steak and a couple of kidneys—becoming a complete meal when baked in a crust.

Pot pies travelled to the New World along with the thrifty colonists, and gradually became regional American fare. They were made with everything from rabbit and game to oysters and ham, though chicken was as popular then as it is now. With the advent of TV dinners and frozen pot pies in the fifties, the homemade version slipped into obscurity. Happily, the recent trend toward traditional home cooking has brought pot pies back in all their glory.

◆ ◆ ◆

◆ POULTRY ◆

Chicken, Ham and Fennel Pot Pies

◆ ◆ ◆

5   cups canned low-salt chicken broth
2   fennel bulbs, halved lengthwise, core discarded, thinly sliced
1¾   pounds skinless boneless chicken breast halves,
       cut into 1-inch pieces
½   cup diced carrot

5   tablespoons unsalted butter
5   tablespoons all purpose flour
2½   cups milk (do not use nonfat or low-fat)
3   tablespoons fresh lemon juice
2   teaspoons fennel seeds, crushed
½   teaspoon (or more) salt
¼   pound thinly sliced country ham, cut into matchstick-size strips

     Pie Crust (see recipe on page 71)

1   egg white, beaten to blend (glaze)

Bring broth to boil in Dutch oven over medium heat. Add fennel; cook 7 minutes. Add chicken and carrot; simmer until fennel, chicken and carrot are tender, about 10 minutes. Pour into strainer set over bowl; reserve broth for another use.

Melt butter in heavy large saucepan over medium-high heat. Add flour; stir 2 minutes. Gradually add milk and whisk until sauce thickens, about 4 minutes. Add lemon juice, fennel seeds and ½ teaspoon salt. Add chicken mixture and ham. Season with salt and pepper. Divide filling among eight 1¼-cup soufflé dishes. Cool.

Roll out pie crust on floured surface to ⅛-inch thickness. Cut out 8 rounds, each measuring ½ to 1 inch larger in diameter than soufflé dishes, gathering dough and rerolling as necessary. Cut out leaf decorations from dough scraps, if desired. Lay 1 dough round over each dish. Press dough overhang firmly to adhere to sides and top rim of dish. If using, brush bottom side of cutouts with water and place on dough; cut slits in dough for steam to escape. *(Can be made 1 day ahead. Cover each with plastic; chill.)*

Preheat oven to 375°F. Place pies on large baking sheet. Brush with glaze. Bake until golden, about 40 minutes.

8 SERVINGS

Pie Crust

3 cups sifted all purpose flour
¾ teaspoon salt
¾ cup (1½ sticks) chilled unsalted butter, cut into pieces
4½ tablespoons chilled vegetable shortening, cut into pieces
6 tablespoons (about) ice water

Combine flour and salt in processor and blend. Add butter and shortening and process, using on/off turns, until mixture resembles coarse meal. Add 4 tablespoons water; blend in. Add enough additional water by tablespoonfuls to form moist clumps. Gather dough into ball; flatten into disk. Wrap in plastic and refrigerate until cold, at least 1 hour or up to 1 day.

MAKES 8 SMALL CRUSTS

Chili-rubbed Chicken with Barbecue Table Mop

◆ ◆ ◆

CHILI RUB
¾ cup chili powder (about 3½ ounces)
3 tablespoons brown sugar
2 teaspoons cayenne pepper

MOP
1 cup hickory barbecue sauce
¾ cup ketchup
⅓ cup orange juice
1 tablespoon soy sauce
1 teaspoon hot pepper sauce (such as Tabasco)
2 3½-pound chickens, quartered, backbones discarded

FOR CHILI RUB: Mix all ingredients in bowl.
FOR MOP: Mix first 5 ingredients in medium bowl. Arrange chicken in single layer on large baking sheet. Season with salt and pepper. Sprinkle chili rub generously on both sides of chicken; press to adhere. Let stand at room temperature 1 hour.
Prepare barbecue (medium-high heat). Place chicken, skin side down, on grill rack away from direct heat. Cover grill and cook chicken until cooked through, turning every 5 minutes and covering grill, about 35 to 40 minutes (chili rub may look slightly burned). Serve hot or warm, passing mop separately.

6 SERVINGS

◆ ◆ ◆

BACKYARD BARBECUE FOR SIX

CHILI-RUBBED CHICKEN WITH
BARBECUE TABLE MOP
(AT LEFT; PICTURED BELOW)

PICNIC POTATO SALAD
(PAGE 158; PICTURED BELOW)

COLESLAW

LEMONADE AND BEER

BAKE-SALE LEMON MERINGUE PIE
(PAGE 178)

Grilled Chicken and Vegetables with Wild Rice

◆ ◆ ◆

1½ cups balsamic vinegar
½ cup olive oil
½ cup honey
⅓ cup chopped fresh oregano or 1½ tablespoons dried
⅓ cup chopped fresh sage or 1½ tablespoons dried
½ teaspoon ground allspice
½ teaspoon ground cumin
8 large skinless boneless chicken breast halves

2 cups (12 ounces) wild rice, cooked according to package directions

2 large red onions, cut into ¾-inch-thick rounds
3 zucchini, trimmed, cut lengthwise into thirds
3 Japanese eggplants, trimmed, cut lengthwise into thirds
2 large red bell peppers, seeded, cut into 1-inch-wide strips

Additional chopped fresh oregano
Additional chopped fresh sage

Combine first 7 ingredients in large glass baking dish. Add chicken, turning to coat. Cover and chill 2 to 4 hours.

Prepare barbecue (medium-high heat). Spread rice in center of large platter. Remove chicken from marinade and sprinkle with salt and pepper. Grill until just cooked through, about 5 minutes per side. Transfer chicken from grill to platter and arrange atop rice.

Add vegetables to marinade and turn to coat. Transfer to barbecue. Sprinkle vegetables with salt and pepper and grill until just cooked through, about 6 minutes per side for onions and 4 minutes per side for zucchini, eggplants and peppers. Transfer vegetables directly from grill to platter and arrange atop rice with chicken. Pour marinade into small saucepan and bring to boil. Brush over chicken; drizzle lightly over grilled vegetables. Sprinkle with additional chopped herbs and serve immediately.

6 SERVINGS

◆ ◆ ◆

MIDWESTERN MENU FOR SIX

CUCUMBER-YOGURT SOUP
(PAGE 26; PICTURED OPPOSITE)

GRILLED CHICKEN AND
VEGETABLES WITH WILD RICE
(AT RIGHT; PICTURED OPPOSITE)

DRY WHITE WINE

MELON AND BLUEBERRY COUPE
WITH WHITE WINE,
VANILLA AND MINT
(PAGE 184; PICTURED OPPOSITE)

SUGAR COOKIES

◆ ◆ ◆

Chicken Curry with Green Apple and Coconut Chutney

◆ ◆ ◆

To prepare the coconut for the chutney, insert an ice pick into the "eyes" and drain the liquid. Bake the coconut until the shell begins to crack. Using a hammer, tap the coconut to remove the shell.

◆ ◆ ◆

CHUTNEY

1   fresh coconut

1   teaspoon cumin seeds

1   pound Granny Smith apples
2   tablespoons fresh lemon juice
½   large bunch cilantro, stemmed
2   serrano or jalapeño chilies, seeded, stemmed, halved
2   garlic cloves, each cut in half
¾   teaspoon salt

CHICKEN CURRY

9   large garlic cloves
2   serrano or jalapeño chilies, stemmed, halved, seeded
1   3-inch-long piece fresh ginger, peeled, coarsely chopped
¼   cup vegetable oil
3   medium onions, finely chopped
5   tablespoons plus 1 cup water
1   4-inch-long cinnamon stick, broken in half
5   whole cardamom pods, cracked
1   teaspoon whole cloves
½   teaspoon whole black peppercorns
3   small bay leaves
3   tablespoons ground coriander
2   tablespoons ground cumin
1   teaspoon cayenne pepper
¼   teaspoon ground turmeric
1   pound tomatoes, minced
1½ teaspoons salt
2   3-pound chickens, each cut into 8 pieces, skinned

3   cups white rice, cooked
¼   cup chopped fresh cilantro

FOR CHUTNEY: Preheat oven to 375°F. Pierce the "eyes" of the coconut with ice pick. Drain off liquid. Bake coconut until shell begins to crack, about 30 minutes. Tap coconut shell all over with hammer to remove shell. (The white meat with its brown skin should fall away

from shell; if it doesn't, use paring knife to release meat.) Using paring knife, cut away and discard brown skin, if desired. Rinse coconut. Coarsely chop enough coconut in processor to measure ¾ cup.

Heat small skillet over medium heat. Add cumin seeds; stir until fragrant, about 3 minutes (do not burn). Transfer seeds to plate; cool. Finely grind seeds in spice grinder or in mortar with pestle.

Core apples; cut into ½-inch pieces. Place apples in medium bowl. Add lemon juice and toss to coat. Combine ¾ cup coconut, cumin, apples and next 4 ingredients in processor. Chop finely.

FOR CHICKEN CURRY: With processor running, drop garlic, chilies and ginger down feed tube and process until minced. Heat oil in large Dutch oven over medium-high heat. Add onions; sauté until brown, adding 2 tablespoons water during last minutes of cooking to prevent burning, about 10 minutes. Add chili mixture and 1 tablespoon water; sauté 3 minutes. Add cinnamon, cardamom, cloves and peppercorns; stir 1 minute. Add 2 tablespoons water, bay leaves, coriander, cumin, cayenne and turmeric; sauté 1 minute. Add tomatoes and salt; cook until almost all liquid evaporates, stirring constantly, about 5 minutes. Add chicken pieces 1 at a time, turning to coat in tomato mixture. Add 1 cup water. Cover; simmer until chicken is cooked through, turning once, about 40 minutes.

Spoon rice onto plates. Top with chicken and sauce. Garnish with chopped cilantro. Serve with chutney.

8 SERVINGS

ABOUT PAELLA

This hearty rice dish, which makes such an impressive party entrée, is in fact a peasant dish from Spain, where its preparation is the focus of many a family celebration. The name of the dish comes from the large, shallow, double-handled pan called a *paellera*, in which it is traditionally cooked outdoors over a charcoal fire.

Like most country recipes, paella is wonderfully versatile, its ingredients easily varied depending on what is seasonal. A traditional peasant paella is as likely to include snails, eels and squid as it is chicken, lamb, sausage and pork. Upscale versions combine lobster, mussels and prawns with rabbit and chicken. Other typical ingredients include artichoke hearts, white beans and vegetables, with garlic, saffron and rosemary as the seasonings of choice.

Traditionally, a short-grain rice from Spain's Valencia region forms the paella base, but it can be difficult to find here. Any short-grain rice can be used with success, with arborio making an excellent substitute.

◆ ◆ ◆

Mountain-Style Paella

◆ ◆ ◆

2	large red bell peppers, seeded
¼	cup olive oil
1	3½-pound chicken, cut into 8 pieces
1½	pounds breakfast pork sausage links, cut into 1-inch pieces
1	pound mushrooms, thinly sliced
3	pounds tomatoes (about 7 cups), chopped
2	tablespoons minced garlic
1	pound green beans, trimmed, cut into 1-inch lengths
½	cup almonds, finely ground
1½	tablespoons chopped fresh rosemary
1½	tablespoons chopped fresh sage
2	teaspoons salt
2	teaspoons ground black pepper
½	teaspoon saffron threads, crushed
¼	teaspoon dried crushed red pepper
2	cups arborio rice or short-grain white rice
6	cups (or more) hot canned low-salt chicken broth
	Lemon wedges

Cut 1 bell pepper lengthwise into thin strips. Chop second pepper; reserve. Heat olive oil in heavy 14-inch skillet or paella pan over

medium-high heat. Add bell pepper strips; sauté until softened, about 6 minutes. Using tongs, transfer pepper strips to bowl; reserve. Season chicken with salt and pepper. Add to skillet and cook until brown on all sides, about 12 minutes. Transfer to plate. Add sausage to skillet; sauté until golden, about 5 minutes. Using slotted spoon, transfer sausage to plate with chicken.

Pour off all but 6 tablespoons drippings from skillet. Add thinly sliced mushrooms to skillet; sauté over medium-high heat 5 minutes. Stir in chopped tomatoes, garlic and chopped bell pepper and bring to boil. Reduce heat and simmer until almost all liquid evaporates, approximately 35 minutes.

Add green beans and next 7 ingredients to skillet. Stir in rice, chicken, sausage and 6 cups hot broth; bring to boil. Reduce heat to medium; simmer uncovered until chicken is cooked, adding more broth if mixture seems dry, about 30 minutes. Let stand 5 minutes. Top with pepper strips. Garnish with lemon.

8 SERVINGS

Grilled Chicken Caesar Salad

◆ ◆ ◆

⅓	cup bottled Caesar salad dressing
2	tablespoons Dijon mustard
2	skinless boneless chicken breast halves
4	½-inch-thick diagonal slices French bread baguette
4	drained canned anchovy fillets
4	cups bite-size pieces romaine lettuce
	Grated Pecorino Romano cheese

Prepare barbecue (medium-high heat) or preheat broiler. Whisk dressing and mustard in small bowl to blend. Reserve ⅓ cup dressing mixture for salad. Brush chicken with remaining mixture; season with salt and pepper. Grill or broil chicken until cooked through, about 4 minutes per side. Transfer chicken to plate. Grill or broil bread until lightly toasted, about 1 minute per side. Transfer toasts to work surface; top each toast with 1 anchovy.

Toss lettuce in medium bowl with reserved ⅓ cup dressing mixture; divide salad between 2 plates. Cut chicken crosswise into thin slices; arrange over lettuce. Sprinkle salads with cheese. Garnish with anchovy toasts and serve.

2 SERVINGS

◆ ◆ ◆

In this heartier version of the classic salad, chicken breasts are grilled, sliced on the diagonal and then arranged atop the lettuce. Grilled slices of French bread topped with anchovies complete the picture.

◆ ◆ ◆

Moroccan Couscous with Chicken and Vegetables

◆ ◆ ◆

1	3½-pound chicken, cut into 6 pieces
4	cups canned chicken broth
3½	tablespoons butter
¼	cup vegetable oil
1	large onion, cut into wedges
½	pound plum tomatoes, quartered
1	cup chopped fresh parsley
1½	teaspoons ground ginger
1½	teaspoons ground black pepper
1	teaspoon ground turmeric
1	whole jalapeño chili
½	cinnamon stick
¼	teaspoon cayenne pepper
⅛	teaspoon saffron threads, crushed
5	small white turnips (about 1¼ pounds), peeled, quartered
4	large carrots, peeled, quartered lengthwise and then crosswise
1	small acorn squash, peeled, seeded, cut into 2-inch pieces
3	zucchini, quartered lengthwise and then crosswise
1	15- to 16-ounce can garbanzo beans (chick-peas)
½	cup raisins

2¼ cups water

1⅓ teaspoons salt

3 cups couscous (about 18 ounces)

Combine chicken and broth in large Dutch oven. Simmer until chicken is cooked through, turning occasionally, about 20 minutes. Using tongs, remove chicken from cooking liquid; reserve cooking liquid. Skin and bone chicken; cut into bite-size pieces. *(Can be made 1 day ahead. Chill chicken and cooking liquid separately.)*

Melt 2 tablespoons butter with oil in heavy large Dutch oven over medium-high heat. Add onion and sauté until tender, about 10 minutes. Add tomatoes and next 8 ingredients and stir 30 seconds. Mix in reserved chicken cooking liquid, turnips, carrots, squash, zucchini, garbanzo beans with liquid and raisins. Cover and simmer until vegetables are tender, about 5 minutes. Add chicken to sauce and cook until heated through, 3 minutes. Discard chili.

Meanwhile, bring 2¼ cups water, 1½ tablespoons butter and salt to boil in medium saucepan. Stir in couscous. Remove from heat, cover and let stand 10 minutes. Fluff with fork.

Arrange couscous in center of serving platter. Drizzle couscous with ¾ cup sauce. Spoon chicken and vegetables atop couscous. Serve, passing remaining sauce separately.

6 SERVINGS

Maple Barbecued Chicken

◆ ◆ ◆

3 tablespoons pure maple syrup

3 tablespoons bottled chili sauce

1 tablespoon cider vinegar

2 teaspoons country-style Dijon mustard

4 skinless boneless chicken thighs

1 tablespoon vegetable oil

Prepare barbecue (medium-high heat). Stir maple syrup, chili sauce, vinegar and mustard in small saucepan until well blended. Brush chicken with oil; season with salt and pepper. Arrange chicken on barbecue. Grill until cooked through, turning occasionally and brushing generously with sauce, about 10 minutes. Serve.

2 SERVINGS

◆ ◆ ◆

MOROCCAN FEAST FOR SIX

OLIVES AND TOASTED ALMONDS

MOROCCAN COUSCOUS WITH
CHICKEN AND VEGETABLES
(AT LEFT; PICTURED OPPOSITE)

LAMB TAGINE WITH ALMONDS
(PAGE 58)

MERLOT

ORANGE BLOSSOM
ALMOND CRESCENTS
(PAGE 217)

PERFUMED ORANGES
(PAGE 185)

MINT TEA
(PAGE 39)

◆ ◆ ◆

Chicken Salad with Greens, Roasted Potatoes and Shallots

❖ ❖ ❖

ROASTED VEGETABLES

2   large russet potatoes, cut into ½-inch cubes

8   large shallots, cut lengthwise into ¼-inch-thick slices

3   tablespoons olive oil

CHICKEN AND SALAD

12   cups mixed baby greens (about 8 ounces)

½   cup all purpose flour

4   skinless boneless chicken breast halves

1   tablespoon olive oil

    Shallot and Mustard Vinaigrette (see recipe below)

FOR ROASTED VEGETABLES: Preheat oven to 450°F. Combine all ingredients in baking pan. Season with salt and pepper. Stir to coat. Bake until cooked through, stirring occasionally, 30 minutes.

FOR CHICKEN AND SALAD: Place greens in large bowl and chill. Place flour in shallow dish. Season with salt and pepper. Coat chicken with flour. Heat oil in heavy large skillet over medium-high heat. Add chicken; cook until done, about 4 minutes per side.

Add roasted vegetables to greens. Add ¼ cup vinaigrette and toss to coat. Divide among plates. Slice chicken on diagonal. Fan chicken atop greens. Drizzle with remaining vinaigrette and serve.

4 SERVINGS

Shallot and Mustard Vinaigrette

1   large shallot, minced

1   tablespoon Dijon mustard

2   tablespoons balsamic vinegar

⅓   cup plus 2 tablespoons olive oil

1½   tablespoons chopped fresh thyme or 1½ teaspoons dried

Combine minced shallot and Dijon mustard in small bowl. Whisk in balsamic vinegar. Gradually whisk in olive oil. Add thyme. Season with salt and pepper. *(Can be prepared 1 day ahead. Cover and refrigerate. Bring to room temperature before using.)*

MAKES ABOUT ½ CUP

❖ ❖ ❖

WARM-WEATHER SALAD SUPPER FOR FOUR

MARINATED ARTICHOKE HEARTS
AND MUSHROOMS

SAGE FOCACCIA
(PAGE 165; PICTURED OPPOSITE)

CHICKEN SALAD WITH GREENS,
ROASTED POTATOES
AND SHALLOTS
(AT LEFT; PICTURED OPPOSITE)

SAUVIGNON BLANC OR
PINOT BLANC

FRUIT WITH CASSIS-SPIKED
LEMON CURD SAUCE
(PAGE 180; PICTURED OPPOSITE)

❖ ❖ ❖

Chicken and Three-Bean Burritos

◆ ◆ ◆

12 large flour tortillas

6 skinless boneless chicken breast halves
Fresh lime juice
Chili powder
Ground cumin
1 tablespoon olive oil

Three-Bean Salad (see recipe below)
2 avocados, peeled, sliced, rinsed under cold water, drained
1 head romaine lettuce, shredded
Grated cheddar cheese
Sour cream or plain yogurt

Preheat oven to 350°F. Wrap tortillas in foil, covering completely. Bake until heated through, about 15 minutes.

Meanwhile, sprinkle chicken with lime juice, chili powder, cumin and salt. Heat oil in large skillet over medium heat. Add chicken; sauté until cooked through, 5 minutes per side. Cut crosswise into strips. Transfer to bowl. Transfer tortillas to cloth-lined basket.

Arrange tortillas, chicken, salad and condiments on table. Allow diners to assemble their own burritos.

6 SERVINGS

Three-Bean Salad

1 15-ounce can yellow hominy, rinsed, drained
1 15-ounce can black beans, rinsed, drained
1 cup drained canned kidney beans, rinsed
1 cup drained canned pinto beans, rinsed
4 large tomatoes, seeded, chopped
1¼ cups chopped red onion
1 cup chopped fresh cilantro
3 tablespoons fresh lime juice
1 tablespoon olive oil
2½ teaspoons chili powder
2½ teaspoons ground cumin

Combine all ingredients in bowl. Season with salt and pepper. *(Can be made 4 hours ahead. Cover and refrigerate.)*

6 SERVINGS

Orange Chicken and Mixed Greens Salad

◆ ◆ ◆

⅔ cup plus ¼ cup fresh orange juice
¼ cup honey
4 large garlic cloves, minced
1 tablespoon minced fresh thyme or 1 teaspoon dried
2 teaspoons grated orange peel
8 boneless chicken breast halves with skin

3 oranges, peel and white pith removed

6 tablespoons olive oil
¼ cup white wine vinegar
1 large shallot, minced
1 pound mixed greens
1 orange or yellow bell pepper, seeded, thinly sliced

Fresh thyme sprigs (optional)

Mix ⅔ cup orange juice, honey, 3 garlic cloves, minced thyme and orange peel in 13 x 9 x 2-inch glass baking dish. Add chicken breasts and turn to coat. Chill overnight, turning occasionally.

Prepare barbecue (medium-high heat) or preheat broiler. Remove chicken from marinade; reserve marinade. Season chicken with salt and pepper. Grill chicken until cooked through, about 4 minutes per side. Transfer to plate.

Boil reserved marinade in heavy small saucepan until reduced to ¼ cup, about 10 minutes. Cut oranges between membranes to release segments. *(Chicken, reduced marinade and orange segments can be prepared 2 hours ahead. Cover separately and store at room temperature. Rewarm marinade before using.)*

Whisk oil, vinegar, shallot and remaining ¼ cup orange juice and garlic clove in small bowl to blend. Season dressing with salt and pepper. Combine greens, bell pepper and orange segments in very large bowl. Toss with dressing. Arrange greens in center of platter.

Cut chicken breasts diagonally into ½-inch-thick slices. Overlap chicken slices around outside edge of platter. Drizzle chicken with marinade. Garnish with thyme sprigs, if desired.

10 SERVINGS

◆ ◆ ◆

GARDEN PARTY FOR TEN

MELON WITH PORT AND MINT

RED ONION, GOAT CHEESE AND BASIL TART
(PAGE 141)

ORANGE CHICKEN AND MIXED GREENS SALAD
(AT LEFT)

BABY SQUASH WITH CAPERS AND PARSLEY
(PAGE 140)

CHARDONNAY

SPARKLING WATER, ICED TEA AND LEMONADE

LEMON BUTTERMILK CAKE WITH STRAWBERRIES
(PAGE 188)

◆ ◆ ◆

Cornish Game Hens with Mustard and Rosemary

◆ ◆ ◆

6 tablespoons butter, room temperature
⅓ cup finely chopped prosciutto
5 teaspoons chopped fresh rosemary
2½ teaspoons Dijon mustard
3 1½-pound Cornish game hens

1½ cups canned chicken broth

1 cup low-fat mayonnaise
3 tablespoons apricot fruit spread

1 bunch watercress

Preheat oven to 400°F. Combine butter, 3 tablespoons prosciutto, 2½ teaspoons rosemary and 1½ teaspoons mustard in bowl. Season with salt and pepper. Run fingers under skin over breast of each game hen, loosening skin from meat. Rub 1 tablespoon butter mixture under skin over breast of each hen. Sprinkle hens inside and out with salt and pepper. Place 1 teaspoon butter mixture in each cavity. Truss hens with kitchen string.

Place hens on rack in large roasting pan. Pour ⅓ cup broth over hens. Dot each hen with 1 teaspoon butter mixture. Roast hens 30 minutes, basting with remaining broth and butter every 10 minutes. Continue roasting without basting until juices run clear when thigh is pierced at thickest part, about 30 minutes more. Reserve ¼ cup pan juices. Cool hens. Cut each hen in half.

Mix mayonnaise, apricot spread, remaining prosciutto, rosemary and mustard, and ¼ cup pan juices in small bowl. (Hens and sauce can be made 1 day ahead. Cover and chill.)

Arrange watercress on large platter. Arrange hens atop watercress. Serve hens immediately with sauce.

6 SERVINGS

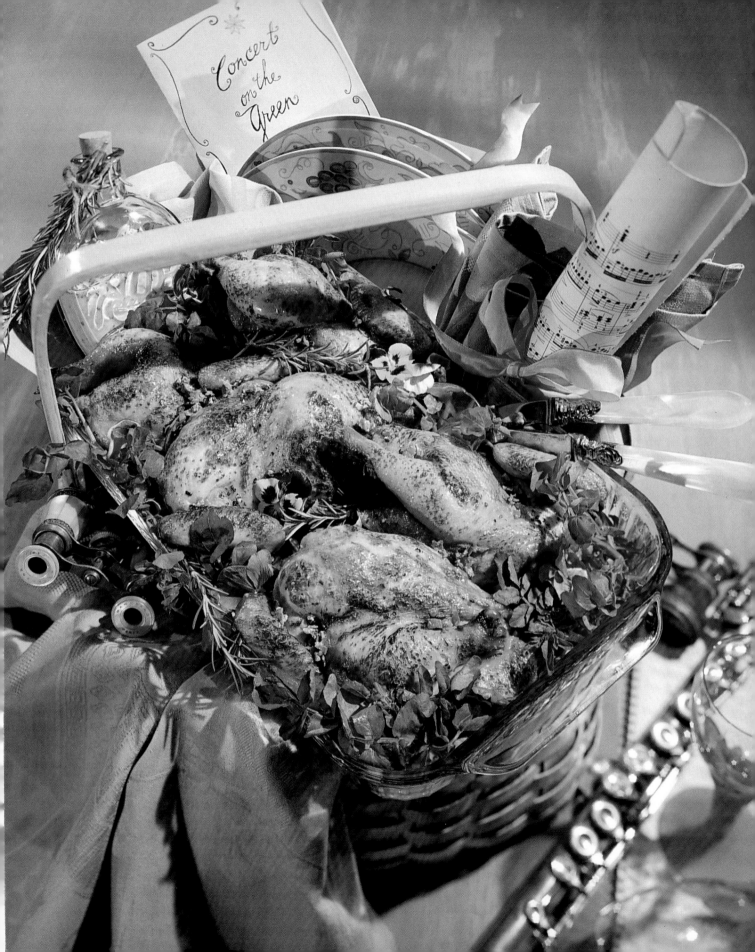

Fricassee of Game Hens with Winter Vegetables and Chestnuts

◆ ◆ ◆

1   red bell pepper

1   cup ½-inch cubes peeled acorn squash
1   cup ½-inch cubes peeled Yukon gold potatoes
1   cup green beans, cut into 1-inch lengths

1   tablespoon plus ½ cup olive oil
4   Cornish game hens, quartered, backs removed
1   cup diced portobello mushrooms (about 2 ounces)
8   cups coarsely chopped greens (such as spinach, arugula, bok choy, kale and/or Swiss chard)
24 vacuum-packed chestnuts*
1   cup cherry tomatoes, halved
2   cups chicken stock or canned low-salt broth

2   tablespoons chopped fresh thyme
2   tablespoons chopped fresh basil

Char pepper over gas flame or under broiler until blackened. Seal in paper bag and let stand 10 minutes. Peel, seed and chop.

Cook acorn squash and potatoes in large pot of boiling salted water 2 minutes. Add green beans and cook 1 minute. Drain. Rinse under cold water. Drain vegetable mixture again.

Heat 1 tablespoon olive oil in heavy large Dutch oven over medium-high heat. Season game hens with salt and pepper. Working in batches, add to Dutch oven and cook until browned on all sides and almost cooked through, turning frequently, about 15 minutes per batch. Transfer game hens to platter. Add diced portobello mushrooms to Dutch oven and sauté 1 minute. Stir in roasted red bell pepper, vegetable mixture, chopped greens, chestnuts and tomatoes. Top with game hens. Pour chicken stock and remaining ½ cup olive oil over. Cover and simmer until game hens are cooked through, stirring occasionally, about 15 minutes.

Transfer game hens to platter. Stir 1 tablespoon thyme and 1 tablespoon basil into vegetable mixture. Season with salt and pepper. Divide vegetable mixture among 4 plates. Top each with 4 game hen pieces. Sprinkle with remaining thyme and basil.

*Vacuum-packed chestnuts are sold at specialty foods stores and in the specialty foods section of some supermarkets.

4 SERVINGS

Turkey Sausage and Vegetable
Frittata Sandwich

◆ ◆ ◆

1	10- to 12-inch round French bread or sheepherder's bread
3	tablespoons olive oil
½	pound spicy Italian turkey sausages, casings removed
1	onion, chopped
2	zucchini, trimmed, diced
1	green bell pepper, diced
1	large tomato, seeded, diced
3	garlic cloves, chopped
¼	cup chopped fresh basil
10	large eggs
⅓	cup freshly grated Parmesan cheese

Cut bread horizontally in half. Cut out soft insides, leaving ½-inch-thick shells. Brush inside of bread shells with 1 tablespoon oil.

Crumble sausage into large nonstick broilerproof skillet. Sauté over medium heat until brown, about 5 minutes. Transfer sausage to bowl. Add onion, zucchini, bell pepper, tomato and garlic to skillet and sauté until vegetables are tender and liquid evaporates, about 9 minutes. Mix in basil. Cool briefly.

Preheat broiler. Beat eggs in large bowl to blend. Season with salt and pepper. Mix in sausage, then vegetable mixture. Heat remaining 2 tablespoons oil in same skillet over medium heat. Pour in egg mixture. Cover and cook until almost set, occasionally lifting edges to allow uncooked eggs to flow underneath, 7 minutes.

Sprinkle top of frittata with Parmesan. Broil until eggs are set in center and golden brown, about 3 minutes. Run spatula around edge of skillet to loosen frittata and slide into bottom shell of bread, pressing to fit. Press top half of bread over. Cut into wedges and serve or wrap in foil and serve within 1 hour.

6 SERVINGS

Smoked Turkey Salad with Cherries and Hazelnuts

◆ ◆ ◆

1¼ pounds smoked turkey breast, diced
1 cup chopped green onions
¾ cup chopped celery
⅓ cup low-fat mayonnaise
3 tablespoons chopped fresh thyme

6 tablespoons olive oil
3 tablespoons white wine vinegar

8 ounces mixed baby greens
2⅓ cups coarsely chopped pitted cherries
½ cup coarsely chopped husked toasted hazelnuts

Mix turkey, green onions, celery, mayonnaise and 2 tablespoons chopped thyme in medium bowl. Season with salt and pepper.

Whisk oil, vinegar and remaining 1 tablespoon chopped thyme in small bowl to blend. Season with salt and pepper.

Toss greens and vinaigrette in large bowl. Divide among plates. Add cherries and nuts to turkey. Place atop greens.

6 SERVINGS

Turkey Leg Osso Buco

◆ ◆ ◆

2 tablespoons olive oil
3 turkey legs (about 2 pounds), skin removed
1 cup chopped carrots
1 cup chopped parsnips
½ cup chopped onion
2 teaspoons minced garlic
3 large fresh thyme sprigs or 1 teaspoon dried
1 bay leaf
1 28-ounce can Italian-style peeled tomatoes
¼ cup chopped fresh parsley
1½ teaspoons chopped orange peel

Preheat oven to 350°F. Heat oil in heavy large Dutch oven over medium-high heat. Season turkey with salt and pepper. Cook until

This version of the time-honored Italian recipe uses turkey legs in place of veal to cut back on the fat. In keeping with tradition, serve it with polenta (here, cut into whimsical crescent-moon shapes), or mashed potatoes. Note that the recipe can be made a day ahead and refrigerated.

♦ ♦ ♦

brown on all sides, about 8 minutes. Transfer to platter. Add carrots, parsnips, onion, 1 teaspoon garlic, thyme and bay leaf to Dutch oven. Sauté until vegetables are almost tender but not brown, about 5 minutes. Return turkey and any accumulated juices to Dutch oven. Stir in tomatoes with their juices, breaking up tomatoes with back of spoon. Bring to boil.

Cover Dutch oven and bake stew in oven until turkey is very tender, about 1 hour 10 minutes. Transfer turkey to work surface; cool slightly. Remove turkey from bones. Discard bones. Cube meat and return to Dutch oven. Discard bay leaf and thyme sprigs. Season with salt and pepper. *(Can be made 1 day ahead. Cover and chill. Bring to simmer before serving.)*

Mix together parsley, orange peel and 1 teaspoon garlic. Ladle osso buco into bowls. Sprinkle with parsley mixture.

6 SERVINGS

Macadamia-crusted Sea Bass with Thai Red Curry Sauce

◆ ◆ ◆

For a restaurant-style presentation, serve the fish on a bed of colorful vegetables and top it with exotic flying-fish roe. The spicy sauce would also be great with shellfish and chicken.

◆ ◆ ◆

1   cup toasted macadamia nuts (about 4 ounces)
2   cups all purpose flour
1   egg, beaten to blend
4   6-ounce sea bass fillets (about 1 inch thick)

¼   cup olive oil

Thai Red Curry Sauce (see recipe below)

Chopped fresh basil
Chopped toasted macadamia nuts

Finely chop nuts with 1 cup flour in processor. Transfer mixture to medium bowl. Place remaining 1 cup flour in another medium bowl. Place beaten egg in shallow bowl. Season fish with salt and pepper. Lightly coat fish with plain flour; shake off excess. Dip fish into egg, then into macadamia nut mixture, coating completely and pressing nuts firmly to adhere to fish.

Heat oil in heavy large skillet over medium heat. Add fish and cook until crusty and cooked through, about 5 minutes per side.

Meanwhile, rewarm curry sauce in heavy medium saucepan over medium heat, stirring sauce occasionally.

Ladle sauce onto 4 plates. Place fish in center. Garnish with chopped basil and toasted macadamia nuts.

4 SERVINGS

Thai Red Curry Sauce

1   tablespoon olive oil
1   large onion, chopped
1   tablespoon Thai red curry base*
3   cups chicken stock or canned low-salt broth
½   cup canned unsweetened coconut milk*
¼   cup fresh lime juice
2   tablespoons fish sauce (nam pla)*
1   garlic clove, minced

2 tablespoons water
1 tablespoon cornstarch
10 large fresh basil leaves

Heat oil in heavy medium saucepan over medium-low heat. Add onion; sauté until translucent, about 5 minutes. Add curry base; stir 1 minute. Add stock and coconut milk. Boil 5 minutes. Stir in lime juice, fish sauce and garlic. Simmer until reduced to 2 cups, about 20 minutes. Mix 2 tablespoons water and 1 tablespoon cornstarch in small bowl until smooth. Whisk into sauce. Simmer until thick, whisking often, about 1 minute. Mix in basil. Working in batches, puree sauce in blender. Season with salt. *(Can be made 1 day ahead. Cover and chill. Before serving, stir in medium saucepan over medium heat until heated through.)*

Available at Asian markets and in some supermarkets.

MAKES ABOUT 2 CUPS

Golden Fish Sticks

◆ ◆ ◆

2½ tablespoons regular or low-fat mayonnaise
1½ tablespoons sweet pickle relish
3 teaspoons fresh lemon juice

2½ cups cornflakes
2 teaspoons grated lemon peel
2 tablespoons (¼ stick) butter, melted
¾ pound white fish fillets (such as orange roughy), cut crosswise into ¾-inch-wide strips

Position rack in top third of oven and preheat to 500°F. Mix mayonnaise, relish and 1½ teaspoons lemon juice in small bowl. Season sauce to taste with salt and pepper.

Grind cornflakes in processor until coarse crumbs form. Transfer to bowl; mix in lemon peel. Mix butter and 1½ teaspoons lemon juice in small bowl. Season fish with salt and pepper. Brush with lemon butter, then dip into cornflake mixture, coating completely. Arrange fish on baking sheet. Sprinkle with any remaining cornflake mixture. Bake fish until cooked through, about 10 minutes. Serve fish sticks immediately with sauce.

2 SERVINGS

Halibut with Swiss Chard and Ginger Cream Sauce

♦ ♦ ♦

6	7-ounce halibut fillets, each about 1½ inches thick by 2 inches wide
	Olive oil
3½	tablespoons minced fresh ginger
2	shallots, minced
1	tablespoon minced garlic
1	cup bottled clam juice
⅔	cup dry white wine
12	large green or red Swiss chard leaves, thick stems removed
1	cup whipping cream

Brush fish with oil. Mix ginger, shallots and garlic in heavy small saucepan. Rub 1 teaspoon ginger mixture over each fish fillet. Add clam juice and wine to remaining ginger mixture in saucepan. Boil mixture until liquid is reduced to ¼ cup, about 15 minutes.

Steam Swiss chard until just tender, about 30 seconds. Transfer chard to strainer and rinse with cold water. Drain. Pat chard dry. Place 1 chard leaf on work surface. Place another leaf next to first, overlapping long sides. Place 1 fish fillet crosswise near 1 end of chard, leaving 2-inch border on short sides of fish. Season fish with salt and pepper. Fold 2 long sides of chard over fish, then roll up fish in chard, enclosing completely. Repeat with remaining chard and fish. *(Can be made 8 hours ahead. Cover ginger mixture and fish separately and refrigerate.)*

Place steaming rack over boiling water in large Dutch oven. Place fish on rack. Cover; steam fish until cooked through, approximately 8 minutes. Transfer fish to plates.

Meanwhile, add cream to ginger mixture in saucepan. Boil until mixture thickens to sauce consistency, about 5 minutes. Spoon sauce around fish. Serve immediately.

6 SERVINGS

♦ ♦ ♦

SOPHISTICATED SUPPER FOR SIX

HALIBUT WITH SWISS CHARD AND
GINGER CREAM SAUCE
(AT LEFT; PICTURED OPPOSITE)

NEW POTATOES WITH BASIL
(PAGE 151; PICTURED OPPOSITE)

STEAMED ASPARAGUS

FRENCH ROLLS

DRY GEWÜRZTRAMINER

CHOCOLATE RASPBERRY TART
(PAGE 174)

♦ ♦ ♦

Sautéed Halibut with White Beans, Orzo and Porcini

◆ ◆ ◆

1   cup dried small white beans

4   large tomatoes
8   large garlic cloves (unpeeled)

2   ounces dried porcini mushrooms*

½   cup orzo (rice-shaped pasta; also called riso)
5   tablespoons plus 2 teaspoons olive oil
1   tablespoon plus 1 teaspoon Sherry wine vinegar
½   cup plus 2 tablespoons mixed chopped fresh herbs

4   6-ounce halibut or other firm white fish fillets

Place white beans in large saucepan. Add enough water to cover by 3 inches. Let beans stand overnight.

Preheat oven to 400°F. Arrange tomatoes and unpeeled garlic cloves in baking pan. Roast until garlic softens and tomato skins blister, about 15 minutes for garlic and about 30 minutes for tomatoes. Peel and coarsely chop tomatoes. Transfer tomatoes to large bowl. Squeeze garlic from skins and mash. Stir garlic into tomatoes.

Place porcini in large glass measuring cup. Pour enough boiling water over mushrooms to cover. Let stand until softened, about 30 minutes. Drain. Chop mushrooms.

Drain white beans and return to pan. Cover generously with water and boil until almost tender, about 45 minutes. Add orzo and cook until orzo and beans are tender, about 10 minutes. Drain. Transfer beans and orzo to large bowl. Stir in tomato and garlic mixture and chopped porcini mushrooms. Whisk 3 tablespoons olive oil and 1 tablespoon vinegar in small bowl to blend. Pour over hot bean and orzo mixture. Stir in ½ cup chopped herbs. Season to taste with salt and pepper. Let bean mixture cool to room temperature.

Heat 2 tablespoons olive oil in heavy large skillet over medium-high heat. Season fish fillets with salt and pepper. Add fish to skillet and sauté until just cooked through, about 3 minutes per side.

Divide bean mixture equally among 4 plates. Using slotted spatula, arrange fish atop bean mixture. Drizzle each fish fillet with ½ teaspoon oil and ¼ teaspoon vinegar. Sprinkle with remaining 2 tablespoons chopped herbs and serve.

*Available at Italian markets and specialty foods stores.

4 SERVINGS

Red Snapper Xaymaca

◆ ◆ ◆

4	6- to 8-ounce red snapper fillets
6	tablespoons (¾ stick) butter, room temperature
½	cup chopped fresh parsley
¼	cup chopped shallots
2	tablespoons chopped fresh thyme
2	teaspoons drained chopped capers
¼	cup grapefruit juice
¼	cup fresh lemon juice
¼	cup orange juice
½	cup bottled clam juice

Preheat oven to 400°F. Butter small baking pan. Place fish in pan. Rub each fillet with ½ tablespoon butter. Season with salt and pepper. Combine parsley, shallots, thyme and capers in bowl. Spoon over fish, pressing gently. Spoon citrus juices around fish. Bake until cooked through, 10 minutes. Transfer to platter; tent with foil.

Pour pan juices into heavy medium skillet. Add clam juice; boil until reduced to ½ cup, about 8 minutes. Remove from heat. Add 4 tablespoons butter; whisk just until melted. Spoon sauce over fish.

4 SERVINGS

This recipe came to us from a restaurant in Jamaica—thus the dish's name. When Columbus landed on Jamaica in 1494, the island was called Xaymaca. For a restaurant-style garnish, top the fish with a steamed julienne of carrots.

◆ ◆ ◆

The salad days of plainly dressed iceberg lettuce are gone. For a time the sole privilege of energetic gardeners or trendy chefs, new varieties of greens are now available in supermarkets. Here are some to look for.

◆ Chervil: A delicate, feathery green with a light licorice flavor.

◆ Chicory: Also known as curly endive; a crisp, bitter green.

◆ Dandelion: Use the pale young leaves of this bitter, grassy green.

◆ Frisée: The sweetest member of the chicory family; mildly bitter.

◆ Mâche: Also known as lamb's lettuce or corn salad; a distinctive, delicately flavored green.

◆ Mesclun: The French name for a mix of tiny, delicate greens that may include arugula, chervil, chickweed, dandelion and red oakleaf lettuce.

◆ Mustard: A member of the cabbage family; the large-lobed green leaves add a pungent flavor.

◆ Red Oakleaf Lettuce: Tender, with a velvety texture, this red green has a distinctive oak leaf shape.

◆ ◆ ◆

Salmon, Mustard Greens and Potatoes with Mustard-Dill Glaze

◆ ◆ ◆

¼   cup Dijon mustard

¼   cup vegetable oil

¼   cup chopped fresh dill

3   tablespoons packed golden brown sugar

½   pound baby new potatoes, cut into ¼-inch-thick slices

2   8-ounce salmon fillets

1   bunch mustard greens, trimmed, cut crosswise into 2-inch-wide strips

Preheat oven to 350°F. Mix first 4 ingredients in small bowl. *(Sauce can be prepared 2 hours ahead. Cover and let stand at room temperature.)* Place potatoes in small bowl. Spoon 1 tablespoon sauce over and toss to coat. Arrange in baking pan. Bake 15 minutes.

Remove pan from oven; push potatoes to sides of pan. Spread each salmon fillet with 2 teaspoons sauce and place in center of baking pan. Bake until salmon is cooked through, about 18 minutes.

Meanwhile, place greens in large skillet. Toss with 2 tablespoons sauce. Stir over medium-high heat until wilted, about 4 minutes. Divide salmon, greens and potatoes between 2 plates. Serve, passing remaining mustard sauce separately.

2 SERVINGS

Tuna Salad with Bell Pepper, Tomato and Egg

◆ ◆ ◆

2   green or red bell peppers

2   medium tomatoes

3   hard-boiled eggs, peeled, quartered

1   6⅛-ounce can tuna packed in water, drained

2   tablespoons drained capers

3   tablespoons olive oil

3   tablespoons fresh lemon juice

Char peppers over gas flame or in broiler until blackened on all sides. Wrap in paper bag and let stand 10 minutes. Peel and seed peppers; cut into strips. Set aside.

Preheat broiler. Place tomatoes on baking sheet. Broil tomatoes until skins begin to split and blacken in spots, turning occasionally, about 4 minutes. Cool. Peel tomatoes. Cut into wedges. Arrange peppers, tomatoes and eggs on platter. Sprinkle with tuna and capers. Mix oil and lemon juice in small bowl. Season to taste with salt and pepper. Drizzle dressing over salad.

4 SERVINGS

Swordfish with Garlic, Lemon and Herb Sauce

◆ ◆ ◆

½	cup extra-virgin olive oil
¼	cup fresh lemon juice
2	tablespoons hot water
6	tablespoons chopped fresh parsley
2	large garlic cloves, finely chopped
1	tablespoon dried oregano
6	6-ounce swordfish fillets, each about 1 inch thick

Prepare barbecue (medium-high heat) or preheat broiler. Whisk oil in top of double boiler over simmering water until heated through. Gradually whisk in lemon juice, then 2 tablespoons hot water. Add parsley, garlic and oregano and cook sauce 5 minutes to blend flavors, whisking frequently. Season sauce to taste with salt and pepper. Remove sauce from over simmering water.

Lightly brush swordfish on both sides with sauce. Season fish with salt and pepper. Grill or broil until just cooked through, about 5 minutes per side. Transfer fish to platter. Spoon remaining sauce over fish and serve immediately.

6 SERVINGS

Grilled Turbot with Asparagus, Artichokes and Tomatoes

◆ ◆ ◆

3	large tomatoes
2	pounds asparagus, trimmed
¼	cup olive oil
2	9-ounce packages frozen artichoke hearts, thawed, patted dry
2	cups chicken stock or canned low-salt broth
1	cup dry white wine
6	fresh thyme sprigs or ½ teaspoon dried
4	garlic cloves, minced
1	large bay leaf
¼	cup chopped fresh chives or green onions
¼	cup chopped fresh parsley
3	tablespoons drained capers
1	tablespoon grated lemon peel
8	6-ounce turbot or sea bass fillets

Blanch tomatoes in pot of boiling water for 20 seconds. Drain. Peel tomatoes. Cut in half; squeeze out seeds. Chop; set aside.

Cook asparagus in large pot of boiling salted water until crisp-tender, about 4 minutes. Drain. Heat oil in heavy large skillet over medium-high heat. Add artichoke hearts and sauté 5 minutes. Add tomatoes, stock, wine, thyme, garlic and bay leaf and bring to boil. Reduce heat and simmer until liquid thickens slightly, about 20 minutes. Add chives, parsley, capers and lemon peel. Season with salt and pepper. Add asparagus and stir to heat through; discard bay leaf.

Meanwhile, prepare barbecue (medium-high heat) or preheat broiler. Season fish with salt and pepper. Grill or broil fish fillets until cooked through, about 5 minutes per side.

Using slotted spoon, divide vegetable mixture among 8 plates. Arrange fish atop vegetables in center of plates. Spoon pan juices over.

8 SERVINGS

Fish Stew with Tomato and Parsley

◆ ◆ ◆

6   tablespoons olive oil
1   cup chopped onion
2   large garlic cloves, chopped
⅔   cup chopped fresh parsley
1   cup chopped tomato (about 1 medium)
1⅓ cups cold water
⅔   cup dry white wine
2   pounds mixed fish fillets (such as sea bass, shark, orange roughy,
     cod and snapper), cut into 2-inch pieces

Heat olive oil in heavy large pot or Dutch oven over medium-high heat. Add chopped onion and garlic and sauté 4 minutes. Add parsley and stir 2 minutes. Add tomato and cook 2 minutes longer. Add 1⅓ cups cold water and dry white wine and simmer 10 minutes to blend flavors. Add fish fillets and simmer until fish is cooked through, about 10 minutes. Season stew to taste with salt and pepper. Ladle into bowls and serve.

4 SERVINGS

◆ ◆ ◆

SOUP SUPPER FOR FOUR

BLANKETED EGGPLANT
(PAGE 13)

FISH STEW WITH TOMATO
AND PARSLEY
(AT LEFT; PICTURED AT LEFT)

BREAD

COFFEE GRANITA
(PAGE 210)

◆ ◆ ◆

Grilled Spiced Sea Bass with Fresh Mango Salsa

◆ ◆ ◆

2   mangoes, peeled, pitted, chopped
1   small red onion, chopped
1   cup chopped fresh cilantro (about 1 large bunch)
2   green jalapeño chilies, seeded, minced
¼   cup fresh lime juice
2   tablespoons olive oil

6   6-ounce sea bass fillets (about 1 inch thick)
    Olive oil
    Fresh lime juice
    Chili powder

Combine first six ingredients in medium bowl. Season salsa with salt and pepper. Set aside.

Place fish in single layer in baking dish. Brush both sides with oil and lime juice. Sprinkle with chili powder.

Prepare barbecue (medium-high heat). Sprinkle fish with salt and grill until cooked through, 4 minutes per side. Serve with salsa.

6 SERVINGS

Scrambled Eggs with Lox and Cream Cheese

◆ ◆ ◆

12   large eggs
½   teaspoon salt
½   teaspoon pepper
3   tablespoons butter
1   8-ounce package well-chilled cream cheese, cut into ½-inch cubes
6   ounces thinly sliced Nova Scotia smoked salmon or lox,
     cut into ½-inch-wide strips
     Chopped fresh chives (optional)

Whisk eggs, salt and pepper in large bowl to blend. Melt butter in large nonstick skillet over medium-high heat. Add eggs. Using wooden spoon, stir until eggs are almost set, about 5 minutes. Gently fold in cheese and salmon and stir just until eggs are set, about 1 minute. Transfer eggs to platter. Sprinkle with chives.

6 SERVINGS

Shellfish Skewers with Equatorial Glazing and Dipping Sauce

◆ ◆ ◆

2   tablespoons peanut oil
2   jalapeño chilies, minced
2   teaspoons minced peeled fresh ginger
1   garlic clove, minced
¾   cup dry white wine
⅓   cup soy sauce
⅓   cup (packed) dark brown sugar
2   teaspoons cornstarch
1   tablespoon fresh lime juice

¼   cup chopped fresh cilantro
24 large uncooked shrimp, peeled, deveined
24 large sea scallops
6   metal skewers

Heat oil in small saucepan over very low heat until warm. Stir in chilies, ginger and garlic. Cover and cook 6 minutes, stirring occasionally (do not brown). Mix wine, soy sauce, sugar and cornstarch in small bowl until cornstarch dissolves. Add to chili mixture; increase heat to medium-high and whisk until mixture comes to boil and thickens slightly. Remove sauce from heat. Transfer to bowl and cool to room temperature. Stir in lime juice. *(Can be made 4 hours ahead. Let stand at room temperature.)*

Prepare barbecue (medium-high heat). Pour ½ cup sauce into small bowl. Add cilantro to remaining sauce; reserve. Alternate 4 shrimp and 4 scallops on each skewer. Brush both sides with ½ cup sauce. Grill just until cooked through, about 3 minutes per side. Transfer to plates. Serve with reserved sauce.

6 SERVINGS

◆ ◆ ◆

PACIFIC RIM MENU FOR SIX

SHELLFISH SKEWERS WITH
EQUATORIAL GLAZING AND
DIPPING SAUCE
(AT LEFT; PICTURED OPPOSITE)

SESAME SOBA NOODLE AND
VEGETABLE SALAD
(PAGE 158; PICTURED OPPOSITE)

ICED TEA AND BEER

GINGER-MACADAMIA BROWNIES
(PAGE 214; PICTURED OPPOSITE)

STRAWBERRIES

◆ ◆ ◆

Scallops with Garlic and Champagne Sauce

12   large garlic cloves, each cut lengthwise in half

4   tablespoons (½ stick) butter
20   large sea scallops
¼   cup pure maple syrup
¼   cup apple cider
¼   cup dry Champagne
3   tablespoons chopped shallots
3   tablespoons chopped fresh chives

Place garlic in small saucepan of water. Bring to boil. Drain. Return garlic to same saucepan. Add fresh water and bring to boil again. Drain garlic and set aside.

Melt 2 tablespoons butter in heavy large skillet over high heat. Season scallops with salt and pepper. Add scallops to skillet; sauté until cooked through, about 3 minutes per side. Using tongs, transfer scallops to platter and tent with foil to keep warm (do not clean skillet). Add garlic, syrup and cider to skillet; boil until liquid is reduced to glaze, about 3 minutes. Add Champagne, shallots and 2 tablespoons chives to skillet; boil until liquid is reduced to sauce consistency, about 4 minutes. Add remaining 2 tablespoons butter; whisk until melted. Season with salt and pepper. Pour sauce over scallops. Sprinkle with remaining 1 tablespoon chives.

4 SERVINGS

Grilled Crab Burgers

6   ounces fresh crabmeat or 1 6-ounce can, drained
1½ cups fresh white breadcrumbs
½   cup chopped green onions
4½ tablespoons mayonnaise
1   teaspoon Old Bay or other seafood seasoning
1   egg yolk
1½ tablespoons Dijon mustard

     Vegetable oil
4   large slices French bread

Mix crabmeat, 1 cup breadcrumbs, green onions, 2 table-spoons mayonnaise and Old Bay seasoning in medium bowl. Season with salt and pepper. Mix in egg yolk. Form mixture into four 2½-inch-diameter patties. Place remaining ½ cup breadcrumbs in shallow bowl. Dip patties into crumbs, coating completely. Mix remaining 2½ tablespoons mayonnaise with mustard in small bowl.

Prepare barbecue (medium-high heat) or preheat broiler. Brush barbecue rack with oil. Grill burgers until golden brown, about 4 minutes per side. Grill bread slices until lightly toasted, about 1 minute per side. Spread toasts with mustard dressing. Top each with crab burger. Serve immediately.

2 SERVINGS

Super-Hot Shrimp Creole

♦ ♦ ♦

2	tablespoons vegetable oil
6	ounces fresh mushrooms, chopped (about 2 cups)
1	medium onion, chopped
1	green bell pepper, chopped
8	large garlic cloves, chopped
2	teaspoons to 2 tablespoons Cajun (Creole) seasoning for seafood
½	to 1½ teaspoons dried crushed red pepper
1	28-ounce can crushed tomatoes with added puree
1	14½-ounce can stewed tomatoes (preferably Cajun style)
1	pound uncooked shrimp, shelled, deveined

Heat oil in heavy large skillet over medium heat. Add mushrooms, onion, green pepper and garlic and sauté until onion is translucent, about 5 minutes. Add Cajun seasoning and crushed red pepper and stir 1 minute. Mix in crushed tomatoes and stewed tomatoes with their juices; simmer until sauce is thick, stirring occasionally, about 15 minutes. Add shrimp and simmer until just cooked through, about 5 minutes. Serve immediately.

4 SERVINGS

♦ ♦ ♦

This is just the ticket for spicy-food aficionados. Serve it over rice—and keep a fire extinguisher nearby. If your taste is a little less adventurous, start with only 2 teaspoons Cajun seasoning and ½ teaspoon dried crushed red pepper flakes; then adjust the heat as the mixture cooks.

♦ ♦ ♦

Clams in Spicy Coconut-Lime Broth

◆ ◆ ◆

1	tablespoon vegetable oil
5	large shallots, chopped
1	tablespoon chopped peeled fresh ginger
1	teaspoon ground turmeric
¼	teaspoon cumin seeds
2	pounds littleneck clams, scrubbed
1½	cups bottled clam juice
1	cup canned unsweetened coconut milk*
1	cup diced canned tomatoes with juices
1	jalapeño chili, seeded, chopped
1	teaspoon grated lime peel
3	tablespoons fresh lime juice
2	green onions, sliced

Heat 1 tablespoon vegetable oil in large Dutch oven over medium heat. Add chopped shallots and sauté until tender, about 3 minutes. Add 1 tablespoon ginger, 1 teaspoon turmeric and ¼ teaspoon cumin and stir 1 minute. Add clams, clam juice, coconut milk, tomatoes with their juices, jalapeño and lime peel and bring to boil. Cover and cook until clams open, about 7 minutes (discard any that do not open). Stir in lime juice. Season to taste with salt and pepper. Transfer clams and sauce to bowl; sprinkle with green onions.

Coconut milk is available at Indian, Southeast Asian and Latin American markets and many supermarkets.

4 SERVINGS

◆ ◆ ◆

AFTER-WORK DINNER FOR SIX

EGG ROLLS

THAI SHRIMP CURRY
(AT RIGHT; PICTURED OPPOSITE)

GEWÜRZTRAMINER OR THAI BEER

SORBET WITH TROPICAL FRUITS

◆ ◆ ◆

Thai Shrimp Curry

◆ ◆ ◆

½	cup chopped onion
3	large shallots, chopped
3	tablespoons chopped lemongrass (from bottom 3 inches of about 5 peeled stalks)
3	tablespoons chopped cilantro stems
3	tablespoons chopped peeled fresh ginger
1	tablespoon turmeric
2	teaspoons ground cumin
1	teaspoon dried crushed red pepper
½	teaspoon grated lime peel

2 cups canned unsweetened coconut milk
2 8-ounce bottles clam juice

2 tablespoons vegetable oil
2 pounds large uncooked shrimp, peeled, deveined
1 head bok choy, white part cut crosswise into ¼-inch-thick slices,
   dark green part cut crosswise into 1-inch-wide slices
1 pound snow peas, stringed
2 3.5-ounce packages enoki mushrooms, trimmed
   Sliced fresh basil
   Cooked rice

Puree first 9 ingredients in processor until paste forms, occasionally scraping sides of bowl. Transfer curry paste to bowl. *(Can be made 4 days ahead. Cover; chill.)*

Boil coconut milk and clam juice in heavy large saucepan until reduced to 2 cups, about 20 minutes. *(Can be prepared 1 day ahead. Cover and refrigerate.)*

Heat oil in heavy large skillet over high heat. Add 6 tablespoons curry paste; stir 1 minute. Add shrimp and sauté until beginning to turn pink, about 2 minutes. Using slotted spoon, transfer shrimp to plate. Add reduced coconut milk mixture to same skillet; boil until mixture coats spoon thickly, stirring occasionally, about 7 minutes. Add white part of bok choy; boil until beginning to soften, about 2 minutes. Add snow peas; stir until crisp-tender, 1 minute. Return shrimp to sauce. Add green part of bok choy and mushrooms; toss until heated through, 5 minutes. Sprinkle with basil. Serve over rice.

6 SERVINGS

◆ ◆ ◆

You might be surprised to find both lemongrass and coconut milk in your local supermarket; but if you don't, look for them at Southeast Asian and Indian markets.

◆ ◆ ◆

Grilled Vegetable Tostadas with Two Salsas

◆ ◆ ◆

TOMATILLO SALSA

2	tablespoons olive oil
1	medium onion, chopped
2	large garlic cloves, minced
1	pound fresh tomatillos, husked, quartered
⅔	cup canned vegetable broth
⅓	cup chopped fresh cilantro
½	teaspoon chili powder
	Hot pepper sauce (such as Tabasco)

TOMATO-CHILI SALSA

2	large dried ancho chilies
1½	pounds tomatoes
2	green onions, finely chopped
3	tablespoons chopped fresh cilantro
1	large garlic clove, minced
¾	teaspoon sugar
½	teaspoon ground cumin

TORTILLAS

3	tablespoons vegetable oil
4	8-inch-diameter flour tortillas

GRILLED VEGETABLES

¾	cup olive oil
6	large garlic cloves, minced
1½	teaspoons chili powder
1¼	teaspoons salt
3	large zucchini, cut on deep diagonal into ¼-inch-thick slices
2	large red bell peppers, seeded, cut into 1-inch-wide strips
1	large eggplant, halved lengthwise, cut crosswise into ¼-inch-thick slices
12	large oyster mushrooms
1	large onion, cut into thin rounds

◆ ◆ ◆

In these meatless tostadas, the vegetables are grilled then piled on crispy tortillas and topped with not one, but two fresh salsas and then guacamole (if you like). The tomatillos for the first salsa are available at Latin American markets and also at some supermarkets, as are the dried ancho chilies in the other salsa.

◆ ◆ ◆

FOR TOMATILLO SALSA: Heat oil in large saucepan over medium-high heat. Add onion and garlic; sauté 5 minutes. Add tomatillos;

sauté 3 minutes. Add broth. Reduce heat, cover and simmer until tomatillos are soft, about 8 minutes.

Blend tomatillo mixture and cilantro in food processor until almost smooth. Transfer to bowl. Mix in chili powder. Season with hot pepper sauce and salt. Cover; chill up to 2 days.

FOR TOMATO-CHILI SALSA: Place chilies in bowl. Cover with hot water. Soak until soft, about 20 minutes. Drain. Cut open; scrape out seeds. Cut off stems and coarsely chop chilies.

Blanch tomatoes in boiling water for 20 seconds. Drain and peel. Cut in half; squeeze out seeds. Chop tomatoes.

Combine chilies and ¾ cup tomatoes in processor; puree until smooth. Transfer to bowl. Mix in remaining tomatoes, chopped green onions, chopped cilantro, garlic, sugar and cumin. Season with salt. Cover salsa and refrigerate up to 1 day.

FOR TORTILLAS: Line baking sheet with paper towels. Heat oil in large skillet over medium-high heat. Add 1 tortilla; fry until crisp and golden, about 30 seconds per side. Transfer tortilla to paper towels and drain. Repeat frying and draining with remaining tortillas.

FOR VEGETABLES: Preheat oven to 350°F. Prepare barbecue (medium-high heat). Mix olive oil, garlic, chili powder and salt in large bowl. Pour ¼ cup oil mixture into small bowl. Add zucchini, bell peppers and eggplant to oil mixture in large bowl; toss to coat.

Grill zucchini, bell peppers and eggplant in batches until light brown, about 3 minutes per side. Place on baking sheet. Cover with foil. Brush mushrooms and onion rounds with reserved ¼ cup oil mixture. Grill until light brown, about 3 minutes per side.

Meanwhile, transfer tortillas to clean baking sheet and rewarm in oven until hot, about 5 minutes. Place 1 tortilla on each plate. Top with vegetables. Serve with salsas.

4 SERVINGS

FLOUR BEYOND ALL PURPOSE

All purpose is the flour most commonly used in everyday baking. But increasingly, different kinds of flour are being added to the mix for extra nutrition, texture and color. Here's a sample of what's available.

◆ Barley Flour: Low in protein but high in minerals, this flour made from hulled barley grains is often used in Middle Eastern breads.

◆ Buckwheat Flour: Milled from buckwheat seeds, this flour is used to flavor breads and pancakes.

◆ Chick-Pea Flour: Often used in Mediterranean and Indian cooking, chick-pea flour is sometimes sold as *gram* or *besan* flour.

◆ Gluten Flour: Wheat is stretched and washed to make this high-protein, low-starch flour.

◆ Semolina Flour: This yellow flour made from durum wheat is used for making pasta and also some Mediterranean breads.

◆ Soy Flour: With four times the protein of ordinary wheat flour, soy flour lends a sweet flavor and crisp texture to breads.

◆ Triticale Flour: Made from a newly developed grain that is a cross between wheat and rye, this flour adds nutrition and texture to different breads.

◆ ◆ ◆

Potato Pancakes with Chick-Pea Flour, Cilantro and Cumin

◆ ◆ ◆

2½ pounds white potatoes, peeled, grated into cold water to cover
1   large white onion, grated
½   cup finely chopped green onion
½   cup chopped fresh cilantro
½   cup chick-pea flour*
2   large eggs, beaten to blend
1½ tablespoons minced seeded jalapeño chili
2   teaspoons ground coriander
1½ teaspoons salt
½   teaspoon ground black pepper
¼   teaspoon cayenne pepper

3   tablespoons (or more) vegetable oil
1½ teaspoons cumin seeds
½   teaspoon ground turmeric

Place grated potatoes and onion in large colander and drain well. Using hands, squeeze mixture to extract as much liquid as possible. Transfer potato mixture to large bowl. Mix in chopped green onion and next 8 ingredients. Set aside.

Heat 2 tablespoons oil in large nonstick skillet over medium-high heat. Add cumin and turmeric and stir 30 seconds. Stir spices into potato mixture in large bowl. Cover and let potato mixture stand 30 minutes to allow flavors to blend.

Preheat oven to 250°F. Heat 1 tablespoon oil in same skillet over medium heat. Add scant 3 tablespoons potato mixture to skillet for each pancake; using spatula, flatten to about 4-inch rounds. Cook until golden, about 5 minutes per side. Transfer pancakes to oven-proof dish; keep warm in oven. Repeat with remaining potato mixture, adding more oil to skillet as necessary. Serve warm.

Available at Middle Eastern and Indian markets.

MAKES ABOUT 18

Portobello Mushroom Burgers with Basil-Mustard Sauce

♦ ♦ ♦

1	cup mayonnaise
⅓	cup chopped fresh basil
2	tablespoons Dijon mustard
1	teaspoon fresh lemon juice
⅓	cup olive oil
1	tablespoon minced garlic
6	4- to 5-inch-diameter portobello mushrooms, stems removed
6	3½- to 4-inch-diameter whole-grain hamburger buns, split
6	large romaine lettuce leaves
6	large tomato slices

Mix first 4 ingredients in small bowl. Season with salt and pepper. Whisk olive oil and garlic in another small bowl.

Prepare barbecue (medium-high heat). Brush mushroom caps on both sides with garlic oil. Season with salt and pepper. Grill mushrooms until tender and golden brown, 4 minutes per side. Transfer to platter; cover with foil. Grill cut side of buns until golden.

Place bottom half of bun on each plate. Top each with 1 mushroom, then 1 lettuce leaf and 1 tomato slice. Spoon some basil-mustard sauce over; top with bun. Serve with remaining sauce.

6 SERVINGS

♦ ♦ ♦

VEGETARIAN MENU FOR SIX

PORTOBELLO MUSHROOM BURGERS WITH BASIL-MUSTARD SAUCE (AT LEFT; PICTURED AT LEFT)

BROWN RICE, CORN AND GRILLED VEGETABLE SALAD (PAGE 155; PICTURED AT LEFT)

ICED HERBAL TEA

NECTARINE COBBLER (PAGE 183)

♦ ♦ ♦

Eggplant, Tomato and Goat Cheese Sandwiches

◆ ◆ ◆

3   tablespoons olive oil
2   large garlic cloves, minced

1   12-inch-long piece baguette, cut horizontally in half
1   small eggplant, cut lengthwise into six ½-inch-thick slices
3   medium tomatoes, cut into 10 slices total

3   ounces soft fresh goat cheese (such as Montrachet)
12   fresh basil leaves

Prepare barbecue (medium-high heat) or preheat broiler. Combine oil and garlic in small bowl. Let stand 5 minutes.

Brush cut sides of baguette and both sides of eggplant slices and tomato slices with garlic oil. Grill cut sides of baguette until toasted, about 2 minutes. Transfer baguette, cut side up, to plates. Season eggplant and tomatoes with salt and pepper. Grill eggplant until cooked through, 6 minutes per side; transfer to plate. Grill tomatoes until warmed through, 1 minute per side; transfer to plate.

Spread goat cheese on bread, dividing equally. Overlap eggplant slices, then tomato slices on baguette halves, covering completely. Garnish with fresh basil leaves. Cut each sandwich diagonally into 4 sections and serve immediately.

2 SERVINGS

Roasted Garlic and Wild Mushroom Risotto

◆ ◆ ◆

2   large heads garlic (about 40 cloves), cloves separated, unpeeled
4   tablespoons olive oil

¾   ounce dried porcini mushrooms*

¾   pound mixed fresh wild mushrooms (such as shiitake and crimini, stems trimmed from shiitake), sliced

1   cup chopped shallots
2   tablespoons chopped fresh thyme or 2 teaspoons dried
1½   cups arborio rice* or medium-grain white rice

½   cup dry white wine
3½ to 4 cups canned low-salt chicken broth or vegetable broth
2   cups thinly sliced fresh spinach leaves
⅓   cup freshly grated Parmesan cheese (about 1 ounce)

Preheat oven to 400°F. Combine garlic and 2 tablespoons oil in small baking dish. Bake until garlic is golden and tender when pierced with small sharp knife, stirring occasionally, about 50 minutes. Cool slightly; peel garlic. Chop enough garlic to measure ¼ cup packed (refrigerate remaining garlic for another use).

Place porcini in small bowl. Pour enough hot water over to cover. Let stand until soft, about 30 minutes. Drain porcini. Squeeze porcini dry and then coarsely chop.

Heat 1 tablespoon oil in nonstick skillet over medium-high heat. Add fresh mushrooms; sauté until juices evaporate, about 7 minutes. Add porcini and stir 1 minute. Season with salt and pepper.

Heat 1 tablespoon oil in heavy medium saucepan over medium-high heat. Add shallots and thyme and sauté until tender, about 4 minutes. Add rice and stir to coat with shallot mixture. Add wine and cook until almost evaporated. Mix in chopped garlic and 3½ cups chicken broth and bring to boil. Reduce heat to medium and cook until rice is tender and mixture is creamy, stirring occasionally and adding more broth if risotto is dry, about 20 minutes. Add mushroom mixture and spinach. Stir until spinach wilts. Stir in Parmesan cheese. Season to taste with salt and pepper.

Dried porcini mushrooms and arborio rice are available at Italian markets, specialty foods stores and some supermarkets.

6 SERVINGS

RISOTTO GOES MAINSTREAM

Once a rarity on American tables, risotto is now a regular part of the culinary repertoire and a standard offering on Italian menus across the country. Inventive chefs have taken the classic recipe—Italian short-grain rice (arborio) slowly simmered in stock and stirred until rich and creamy—and made it their own, adding everything from wild mushrooms and roasted garlic (see the version at left) to shrimp and basil. Like pasta, risotto is wonderfully versatile.

The dish originated in Northern Italy, near the fertile Po Valley. Over time, as its popularity spread, different cities and regions—and today, even different restaurants—have claimed their own favorite version of risotto. Venetian-style risotto is slightly soupy. Risotto *alla milanese*, is drier (the excess liquid having been allowed to evaporate) and especially creamy.

Newest on the risotto front are other grains and pastas being prepared using the same slow-cooking and stirring method. You'll find risotto-like couscous, barley and orzo (rice-shaped pasta), even risotto-like potatoes, made with diced potatoes.

◆ ◆ ◆

THE MEATLESS MOVEMENT

With more and more people eating meatless meals occasionally if not all the time, foods high in complex carbohydrates—grains, beans and pasta—have taken on starring roles in many deliciously imaginative entrées.

Nutritionists recommend that carbohydrates be the cornerstone of a healthful diet. Beans are one of the most nutritional foods around. By way of example, a six-ounce cup of cooked white beans provides 15 grams of protein—about a quarter of the recommended daily allowance—and contains just 200 calories and only a single gram of fat. At a few pennies a serving, beans are also an economical way to get a good dose of iron, folic acid, zinc and fiber.

Other complex carbohydrates, such as grains, pasta and rice, provide great nutritional value, especially when they're paired with lots of vegetables, which add crunch, color, more fiber and more nutrients. A few seasonings stirred into the mix, and you won't miss the meat at all.

◆ ◆ ◆

Poached Eggs with Yogurt and Spicy Sage Butter

◆ ◆ ◆

1   cup plain yogurt
2   large garlic cloves, pressed

¼   cup (½ stick) unsalted butter
12   fresh sage leaves
½   teaspoon paprika
¼   teaspoon dried crushed red pepper

1   tablespoon distilled white vinegar
8   eggs

     Warm pita bread

Stir yogurt and garlic in small bowl to blend. Season with salt. Divide mixture among 4 plates, spreading to coat center.

Melt butter in heavy small saucepan over medium heat. Add sage, paprika and red pepper and stir just until butter sizzles. Remove from heat. Season with salt.

Add vinegar to large skillet of simmering water and return mixture to simmer. Crack eggs into water. Simmer until eggs are softly cooked, about 3 minutes. Using slotted spoon, remove eggs from water, drain briefly and place 2 eggs atop yogurt on each plate.

Rewarm butter mixture if necessary; spoon over eggs and serve immediately with pita bread.

4 SERVINGS

Rice Pancake with Chunky Tex-Mex Sauce

◆ ◆ ◆

3   cups water
1½   cups medium-grain or short-grain white rice
½   cup grated Monterey Jack cheese
1   tablespoon minced seeded jalapeño chili

8   green onions, white and green parts chopped separately
1   15- to 16-ounce can black beans, rinsed, drained
1   14½- to 16-ounce can diced peeled tomatoes
2   teaspoons chili powder

<table>
</table>

1	11-ounce can corn kernels, drained, or ¾ cup frozen corn kernels, thawed
4	tablespoons chopped fresh cilantro
1	large egg, beaten to blend
1	tablespoon vegetable oil

Combine 3 cups water and rice in heavy medium saucepan; bring to boil. Reduce heat to low; cover and cook until water is absorbed and rice is tender, about 20 minutes. Remove from heat. Stir in cheese and jalapeño chili; cool.

Combine white parts of green onions, beans, tomatoes with their juices and chili powder in medium saucepan; bring to boil. Reduce heat; simmer until mixture thickens, about 10 minutes. Add green parts of green onions, corn and 2 tablespoons cilantro. Season with salt and pepper. *(Rice mixture and sauce can be prepared 4 hours ahead. Let stand at room temperature. Rewarm sauce before serving.)* Mix beaten egg into rice mixture.

Heat oil in 12-inch nonstick skillet over high heat. Add rice mixture to skillet. Using spatula, press into even layer, covering bottom of skillet completely. Reduce heat to medium; cover and cook until bottom of pancake is brown and crisp, about 10 minutes. Turn out pancake onto platter, brown side up.

Spoon sauce over pancake. Garnish with remaining 2 tablespoons cilantro. Cut into wedges to serve.

4 SERVINGS

Garden Vegetable Lasagne

◆ ◆ ◆

1 cup bottled marinara sauce, preferably spicy
1 cup coarsely chopped seeded plum tomatoes
1 medium zucchini, thinly sliced
¼ cup chopped fresh basil leaves or 1 tablespoon dried

1 cup low-fat ricotta cheese
8 tablespoons freshly grated Parmesan cheese
3 lasagne noodles

Additional freshly grated Parmesan cheese

Preheat oven to 450°F. Simmer marinara sauce, tomatoes, zucchini and basil in heavy medium saucepan over medium heat until zucchini is tender, stirring occasionally, about 8 minutes.

Meanwhile, mix ricotta cheese and 6 tablespoons Parmesan cheese in bowl to blend; season with salt and pepper. Cook lasagne noodles in pot of boiling salted water until tender but still firm to bite; drain. Cut noodles in half crosswise, making 6 pieces.

Set aside 2 tablespoons vegetable sauce for topping. Place 2 noodle pieces in buttered 8 x 8 x 2-inch glass baking dish, spacing apart. Spread ¼ of cheese mixture, then ¼ of sauce over each. Repeat layering of noodle pieces, cheese mixture and sauce. Top each with another noodle piece, 1 tablespoon reserved sauce, then 1 tablespoon grated Parmesan cheese.

Bake lasagne uncovered until heated through, about 10 minutes. Serve with additional Parmesan cheese.

2 SERVINGS

◆ ◆ ◆

This isn't your mother's lasagne. To begin with, it's missing the meat, with fresh vegetables substituting nicely. And then there's the fact that the recipe shouldn't take you more than 30 minutes, beginning to end. A modern-day masterpiece.

◆ ◆ ◆

Vegetable Ragout with Cumin and Ginger

◆ ◆ ◆

2 tablespoons olive oil
2 cups thinly sliced onions
1 cup sliced carrot
½ cup sliced fennel or celery
1 cinnamon stick
½ teaspoon ground cumin
½ teaspoon ground ginger
½ teaspoon ground turmeric
1 large pinch saffron threads, crushed
2 cups diced peeled russet potatoes
1 cup canned low-salt chicken broth or vegetable broth
2 tablespoons raisins
1 15- to 16-ounce can garbanzo beans (chick-peas), drained
1 medium zucchini, halved lengthwise, cut crosswise
   into ½-inch-thick pieces
½ cup diced seeded tomatoes
2 tablespoons sliced almonds, toasted (optional)

Heat oil in heavy large Dutch oven over medium-low heat. Add onions, carrot, fennel, cinnamon stick, cumin, ginger, turmeric and saffron; sauté until vegetables begin to soften, about 10 minutes. Add potatoes, broth and raisins; bring to boil. Reduce heat to medium-low; cover and simmer until potatoes are almost tender, about 10 minutes. Add garbanzo beans, zucchini and tomatoes; cover and simmer until zucchini is tender, about 8 minutes longer. Transfer ragout to bowl. Sprinkle with almonds, if desired.

4 SERVINGS

◆ PASTA & PIZZA ◆

Buckwheat Pasta Primavera
◆ ◆ ◆

2½   cups canned low-salt chicken broth or water
1   ounce dried shiitake mushrooms
12   sun-dried tomatoes (not packed in oil; about 1 ounce)
1   large carrot, peeled, cut into matchstick-size strips (about 1½ cups)
8   ounces sugar snap peas, trimmed

2   tablespoons (¼ stick) butter
1   large onion, sliced
1   yellow bell pepper, cut into strips
4   garlic cloves, minced
¼   cup whipping cream

12   ounces dried buckwheat pasta (fancy soba)*
1   cup freshly grated Parmesan cheese (about 2 ounces)
2   green onions, sliced
      Additional freshly grated Parmesan cheese

Bring broth to simmer in heavy medium saucepan. Rinse mushrooms briefly under cold water. Add mushrooms and sun-dried tomatoes to broth; simmer until tender, about 4 minutes. Using slotted spoon, transfer mushrooms and tomatoes to plate; cool. Add carrot and sugar snap peas to broth and cook until crisp-tender, about 3 minutes. Using slotted spoon, transfer vegetables to another plate. Boil broth remaining in saucepan until reduced to ¼ cup, about 5 minutes. Reserve broth. Discard mushroom stems. Slice mushroom caps and tomatoes. Set vegetables aside.

Melt butter in heavy large skillet over medium-high heat. Add onion; sauté until tender and golden, about 8 minutes. Add bell pepper and garlic; stir until bell pepper is tender, about 4 minutes. Add carrot, sugar snap peas, mushrooms, tomatoes, reserved broth and cream and bring to boil. Season with salt and pepper.

Meanwhile, cook pasta in large pot of boiling salted water until tender but still firm to bite, about 4 minutes. Drain. Place pasta in large bowl. Pour vegetables and sauce over pasta. Sprinkle with 1 cup Parmesan; toss to coat. Garnish with green onions. Serve, passing additional Parmesan separately.

*Available at Asian markets and in many supermarkets.

4 SERVINGS

Greek-Style Pasta with Shrimp

◆ ◆ ◆

¼   cup olive oil

4   teaspoons minced garlic

1   pound uncooked medium shrimp, peeled, deveined

1½ cups drained canned artichoke hearts, chopped

1½ cups crumbled feta cheese

½   cup chopped seeded tomatoes

3   tablespoons fresh lemon juice

3   tablespoons chopped fresh parsley

2   tablespoons finely chopped fresh oregano or 1½ teaspoons dried

12 ounces angel hair pasta or linguine

Heat oil in heavy large skillet over medium-high heat. Add garlic and sauté 30 seconds. Add shrimp and sauté until almost cooked through, about 2 minutes. Add artichokes, feta, tomatoes, lemon juice, parsley and oregano and sauté until shrimp are cooked through, about 2 minutes. Season with salt and pepper.

Meanwhile, cook pasta in large pot of boiling salted water until just tender but still firm to bite, stirring occasionally. Drain pasta. Transfer pasta to large serving bowl.

Add shrimp mixture to pasta and toss to coat. Season to taste with salt and pepper and serve immediately.

4 SERVINGS

Spaghetti Syracuse Style

◆ ◆ ◆

1   1- to 1¼-pound eggplant, cut into ½-inch cubes
1   large yellow bell pepper
2   pounds tomatoes

½   cup olive oil
2   large garlic cloves, flattened
4   anchovy fillets, chopped
4   ounces brine-cured black olives (such as Kalamata), pitted, coarsely chopped
12 large basil leaves, finely chopped
2   tablespoons drained capers

1   pound spaghetti
½   cup packed freshly grated Pecorino Romano cheese

Arrange eggplant on double thickness of paper towels. Sprinkle with salt. Let stand 30 minutes. Pat eggplant dry with paper towels. Char bell pepper over gas flame or in broiler until blackened on all sides. Wrap in paper bag and let stand 10 minutes. Peel, seed and slice pepper into thin strips. Blanch tomatoes in pot of boiling water for 20 seconds. Drain. Peel tomatoes. Cut tomatoes in half; squeeze out seeds. Chop tomatoes; set aside.

Heat olive oil in large pot or Dutch oven over medium-high heat. Add garlic; sauté until light brown, about 3 minutes. Discard garlic. Add eggplant to pot; sauté until beginning to brown, about 10 minutes. Add anchovies; stir 2 minutes. Add tomatoes; reduce heat to medium and simmer 10 minutes. Add olives, basil, capers and bell pepper strips and simmer until sauce thickens, about 20 minutes. Season with salt and pepper. *(Can be made 1 day ahead. Cover; chill. Rewarm over low heat before using.)*

Cook spaghetti in large pot of boiling salted water until just tender but still firm to bite. Drain well. Transfer spaghetti to large shallow bowl. Spoon sauce over. Sprinkle with cheese.

6 SERVINGS

◆ ◆ ◆

SICILIAN SUPPER FOR SIX

SPAGHETTI SYRACUSE STYLE
(AT LEFT)

SWORDFISH WITH GARLIC, LEMON
AND HERB SAUCE
(PAGE 97)

"DROWNED" BROCCOLI
(PAGE 146)

ITALIAN BREAD

SICILIAN WHITE WINE

CANNOLI

◆ ◆ ◆

Perciatelli with Greens and Seasoned Breadcrumbs

♦ ♦ ♦

SEASONED BREADCRUMBS

3 tablespoons olive oil

2 cups fresh breadcrumbs from French or Italian bread

1 cup freshly grated Pecorino Romano cheese (about 3 ounces)

1 tablespoon grated lemon peel

1 tablespoon dried oregano

PASTA

1 pound perciatelli pasta or spaghetti

4 tablespoons olive oil

4 garlic cloves, chopped

3 bunches greens (such as kale, mustard and/or dandelion), stemmed, sliced crosswise

FOR SEASONED BREADCRUMBS: Heat oil in heavy large skillet over medium-high heat. Add breadcrumbs; stir until crisp and golden, about 3 minutes. Transfer to bowl. Mix in ½ cup cheese, lemon peel and oregano. *(Breadcrumbs can be made 4 hours ahead. Cover and let stand at room temperature.)*

FOR PASTA: Cook pasta in large pot of boiling salted water until tender but still firm to bite, stirring occasionally.

Meanwhile, heat 3 tablespoons oil in large Dutch oven over medium-high heat. Add garlic; stir until light brown, about 1 minute. Add kale, if using, and stir until wilted, 1 minute. Add mustard and/or dandelion greens and stir until wilted, 2 minutes.

Drain pasta, reserving 1½ cups cooking liquid. Return pasta to pot. Add 1 tablespoon oil, greens and reserved cooking liquid; toss to coat. Add remaining ½ cup cheese. Season with salt and generous amount of pepper. Transfer to bowl. Top with breadcrumbs.

4 SERVINGS

♦ ♦ ♦

MEATLESS MENU FOR FOUR

PORCINI AND WHITE BEAN SOUP
(PAGE 32; PICTURED OPPOSITE)

PERCIATELLI WITH GREENS AND
SEASONED BREADCRUMBS
(AT LEFT; PICTURED OPPOSITE)

PINOT GRIGIO

ORANGE AND CINNAMON BISCOTTI
(PAGE 214; PICTURED OPPOSITE)

FRESH PEARS

VIN SANTO OR OTHER ITALIAN
DESSERT WINE

ESPRESSO

♦ ♦ ♦

Penne with Tomatoes, Olives and Two Cheeses

♦ ♦ ♦

6	tablespoons olive oil
1½	cups chopped onion
1	teaspoon minced garlic
3	28-ounce cans Italian plum tomatoes, drained
2	teaspoons dried basil
1½	teaspoons dried crushed red pepper
2	cups canned low-salt chicken broth
1	pound penne or rigatoni
2½	cups packed grated Havarti cheese
⅓	cup sliced pitted brine-cured olives (such as Kalamata)
⅓	cup grated Parmesan cheese
¼	cup finely chopped fresh basil

Heat 3 tablespoons oil in heavy large Dutch oven over medium-high heat. Add onion and garlic; sauté until onion is translucent, about 5 minutes. Mix in tomatoes, dried basil and crushed red pepper. Bring to boil, breaking up tomatoes with back of spoon. Add broth; bring to boil. Reduce heat to medium; simmer until mixture thickens to chunky sauce and is reduced to 6 cups, stirring occasionally, about 1 hour 10 minutes. Season with salt and pepper. *(Can be prepared 2 days ahead. Cover and refrigerate. Rewarm sauce over low heat before continuing with recipe.)*

Preheat oven to 375°F. Cook pasta in large pot of boiling salted water until tender but still firm to bite. Drain well. Return pasta to same pot. Toss with 3 tablespoons oil. Pour sauce over and toss to blend. Mix in Havarti cheese. Transfer pasta to 13 x 9 x 2-inch glass baking dish. Sprinkle with olives, then Parmesan.

Bake until pasta is heated through, about 30 minutes. Sprinkle with chopped basil. Serve immediately.

4 SERVINGS

Orecchiette with Broccoli Rabe

◆ ◆ ◆

¼ cup olive oil
4 garlic cloves, minced

12 ounces orecchiette or shell pasta
1 pound broccoli rabe,* trimmed, chopped
⅔ cup freshly grated Pecorino Romano cheese (about 2 ounces)
⅓ cup freshly grated Parmesan cheese (about 1 ounce)

Heat oil in heavy small saucepan over medium heat. Add garlic and sauté until beginning to color, about 1 minute.

Cook pasta in large pot of boiling salted water until beginning to soften, stirring occasionally, about 8 minutes. Add broccoli rabe and cook until pasta is just tender but still firm to bite, about 3 minutes. Drain. Transfer pasta and broccoli rabe to large bowl. Pour garlic oil over. Sprinkle with cheeses and toss to coat. Season to taste with salt and pepper. Serve immediately.

Broccoli rabe, a member of the cabbage family, is a type of leafy green available in specialty foods stores and some supermarkets.

6 SERVINGS

THE NEW PASTAS

First there was spaghetti, and then there was agnolotti, orcchiette...all sorts of different pastas, some 300 of them to be exact. Here's what's what among what's new and hot.

◆ Agnolotti: Half-moon-shaped, stuffed pasta; served with a sauce made from the meat in the filling.

◆ Bucatini: Long, thick, hollow noodles; excellent with traditional spaghetti sauces.

◆ Cappelletti: Stuffed "little hats"; filled with everything from cheese to pureed pumpkin.

◆ Caramelle: Looking like wrapped candy, this stuffed pasta has a little twist at each end.

◆ Cavatelli: Small, shell pasta with curled edges; good with cheese sauces and in soups or salads.

◆ Orecchiette: "Little ears" from southern Italy; eaten with meat, fish or vegetables.

◆ Perciatelli: Hollow Sicilian spaghetti; goes well with vegetable and seafood sauces.

◆ Ruote de carro: Cartwheels with spokes; good with heavier meat and vegetable sauces.

◆ ◆ ◆

Linguine with Clams and Wild Mushrooms

♦ ♦ ♦

6 tablespoons olive oil
1 pound mixed fresh wild mushrooms (such as oyster mushrooms and shiitake, stems trimmed, caps sliced)
6 large garlic cloves, minced
¼ teaspoon dried crushed red pepper
1 cup dry white wine
5 pounds clams (about 24 littleneck)

1 pound linguine

2 bunches fresh chives or 1 bunch green onions, chopped

Heat 3 tablespoons oil in heavy large Dutch oven over high heat. Add mushrooms and sauté until beginning to brown, about 5 minutes. Using slotted spoon, transfer mushrooms to plate. Add remaining 3 tablespoons oil and garlic to Dutch oven. Sauté until garlic is tender, about 3 minutes. Add crushed red pepper, then wine and clams. Cover and cook until clams open, about 8 minutes.

Meanwhile, cook linguine in large pot of boiling salted water until just tender but still firm to bite.

Drain pasta well and transfer to large bowl. Spoon mushrooms over, then top with clam mixture, discarding any clams that do not open. Season to taste with salt and pepper. Sprinkle with chives.

4 SERVINGS

Rigatoni with Asparagus, Artichokes and Peppers

◆ ◆ ◆

3   large red bell peppers

1½ pounds rigatoni
1½ pounds asparagus, trimmed, cut into 2-inch pieces
1   9-ounce package frozen artichoke hearts, thawed,
     cut lengthwise in half
1   tablespoon olive oil

4½ tablespoons butter
6½ tablespoons all purpose flour
4½ cups milk
2¼ cups packed grated Fontina cheese (about 9 ounces)
3   cups coarsely grated Parmesan cheese (about 6 ounces)

2   ½-ounce packages arugula, coarsely chopped

Char peppers over gas flame or under broiler until blackened on all sides. Wrap in paper bag and let stand 10 minutes. Peel and seed peppers. Cut into ½-inch pieces.

Butter 15 x 10 x 2-inch glass baking dish. Bring large pot of salted water to boil. Add pasta and boil 10 minutes. Add asparagus and artichokes and cook until pasta is tender but still firm to bite, about 4 minutes longer. Drain well. Transfer to large bowl. Add olive oil and toss pasta mixture to coat.

Melt butter in heavy large saucepan over medium-high heat. Add flour and stir 2 minutes. Gradually add milk, whisking until smooth. Cook until sauce thickens, whisking frequently, about 8 minutes. Remove from heat. Add Fontina and 2¼ cups Parmesan cheese and whisk until cheeses melt and sauce is smooth. Season cheese sauce to taste with salt and pepper.

Add cheese sauce, arugula and peppers to pasta and vegetables and stir to coat. Transfer to prepared baking dish. Sprinkle with ¾ cup Parmesan. Cover with foil. *(Can be prepared 1 day ahead; chill. Let stand at room temperature 1 hour before continuing.)*

Preheat oven to 350°F. Bake pasta covered until heated through, about 50 minutes. Uncover and bake until top is glazed, about 10 minutes longer. Serve immediately.

8 SERVINGS

LATE-NIGHT SUPPER FOR EIGHT

ANTIPASTO PLATTER

RIGATONI WITH ASPARAGUS,
ARTICHOKES AND PEPPERS
(AT RIGHT; PICTURED ABOVE)

CHIANTI

COFFEE GELATO

BISCOTTI

◆ ◆ ◆

Trenette with Pesto, Potatoes and Green Beans

◆ ◆ ◆

1   cup packed fresh basil leaves (about 2 bunches)
½   cup olive oil (preferably extra-virgin)
6   tablespoons freshly grated Pecorino Romano cheese (about 1 ounce)
6   tablespoons freshly grated Parmesan cheese (about 1 ounce)
¼   cup pine nuts, toasted
1½   teaspoons minced garlic

2   medium russet potatoes (¾ pound), peeled, cut into ½-inch cubes
6   ounces green beans, trimmed, cut into 3-inch lengths
1   pound trenette pasta or linguine

      Additional freshly grated Pecorino Romano cheese

Finely grind basil, oil, 6 tablespoons each Romano and Parmesan cheeses, toasted pine nuts and minced garlic in processor. Season pesto to taste with salt and pepper. *(Pesto can be prepared 2 days ahead. Press plastic wrap onto surface of pesto and refrigerate.)*

Cook potatoes in large pot of boiling salted water until just tender, about 5 minutes. Using slotted spoon, transfer potatoes to large bowl. Add green beans to same pot and cook until crisp-tender, about 3 minutes. Using slotted spoon, transfer to bowl with potatoes. Cook pasta in same pot until tender but still firm to bite. Drain, reserving ½ cup cooking liquid. Transfer pasta to bowl with potatoes and green beans. Set pasta mixture aside.

Whisk reserved ½ cup cooking liquid into pesto. Add pesto to pasta mixture and toss thoroughly to coat. Transfer pasta to large platter. Serve, passing additional Pecorino Romano separately.

4 SERVINGS

Trenette is a ribbon pasta used often in the cooking of Liguria. The more readily available linguine works equally well in this dish of noodles, potatoes and green beans tossed with a homemade pesto sauce.

◆ ◆ ◆

Pasta with Ricotta and Fresh Herbs

◆ ◆ ◆

1	15-ounce container low-fat ricotta cheese
⅔	cup nonfat milk
½	cup freshly grated Parmesan cheese
2	teaspoons olive oil
1	cup chopped onion
2	garlic cloves, chopped
½	cup chopped fresh basil
¼	cup chopped fresh chives or green onions
¼	cup chopped fresh parsley
12	ounces rotelle or fusilli pasta, freshly cooked

Blend ricotta cheese, milk and Parmesan in processor until smooth. Heat oil in heavy large skillet over medium heat. Add onion; sauté until beginning to brown, about 5 minutes. Add garlic and sauté 2 minutes. Add ricotta mixture, basil, chives and parsley to skillet; stir until heated through, about 5 minutes. Mix in rotelle. Season with salt and pepper and serve.

4 SERVINGS

Pasta with Lobster, Tomatoes and "Herbes de Maquis"

◆ ◆ ◆

The parts of Corsica that are not cultivated or forested are covered with a thick underbrush called the *maquis*. It consists of diverse aromatic herbs; a blend of these herbs, called *herbes de maquis*, is a flavoring for many local seafood specialties, including this rich dish. (For reasons of food safety, it is essential to make the tomato sauce and finish cooking the lobster immediately after the lobster has been boiled.)

◆ ◆ ◆

1	28-ounce can Italian-style tomatoes, drained, juices reserved
2	live lobsters (about 1¼ pounds each)
3	tablespoons extra-virgin olive oil
1	medium onion, minced
2	garlic cloves, minced
1	tablespoon red wine vinegar
2	tablespoons minced fresh basil
1½	teaspoons minced fresh mint
¾	teaspoon minced fresh oregano
¾	teaspoon minced fresh thyme
¾	teaspoon minced fresh rosemary
¼	teaspoon cayenne pepper
⅓	cup whipping cream
1	pound pasta (such as penne or fettuccine)

Chop tomatoes. Bring large pot of water to boil. Add lobsters; boil 2 minutes. Using tongs, transfer lobsters to cutting board. Cut off claws and crack open. Remove meat from claws and cut meat into bite-size pieces. Cut off lobster tails. Cut tails crosswise into 4 pieces each. Cut each lobster body lengthwise in half. Remove coral (orange part) and tomalley (greenish part); finely chop.

Heat oil in Dutch oven over medium heat. Add lobster body pieces (not tails or claw meat), onion and garlic; sauté until onion is soft, about 10 minutes. Add lobster tail pieces, claw meat, coral, tomalley, tomatoes and reserved juices, vinegar, herbs and cayenne; bring to boil. Reduce heat; simmer until lobster is cooked through, about 8 minutes. Using slotted spoon, remove lobster tail pieces and claw meat and reserve. Add cream to sauce. Simmer 20 minutes. Using tongs, remove lobster body pieces and discard. Season sauce to taste with salt and pepper. Set aside.

Meanwhile, cook pasta in pot of boiling salted water until just tender but still firm to bite.

Drain pasta and return to pot. Add lobster and sauce and toss to coat. Divide among plates and serve.

6 SERVINGS

Beef and Chard Ravioli with Sage Butter Sauce

❖ ❖ ❖

❖ ❖ ❖

In this simplified version of ravioli, *gyoza* (potsticker) wrappers are used instead of homemade dough. They are available at Asian markets, and also in the refrigerated section of many supermarkets. If you can't find them, substitute wonton wrappers.

❖ ❖ ❖

1   tablespoon olive oil
3   ounces skirt steak, finely chopped
⅓   cup finely chopped onion
1   garlic clove, minced
1   large bunch Swiss chard, rinsed, stemmed, thinly sliced
1¾   cups beef stock or canned broth
½   cup dry red wine
¼   cup freshly grated Parmesan cheese
     Pinch of ground nutmeg
1   egg yolk, beaten to blend

40   gyoza (potsticker) wrappers
1   egg, beaten to blend

5   tablespoons unsalted butter
5   teaspoons minced fresh sage

Heat olive oil in heavy large skillet over medium-high heat. Add chopped skirt steak, chopped onion and minced garlic and sauté 5 minutes. Add sliced Swiss chard, ¼ cup stock and ¼ cup red wine and simmer until chard wilts and no liquid remains in skillet, about 5 minutes. Transfer mixture to bowl and cool. Mix in Parmesan and nutmeg. Season with salt and pepper. Mix in yolk.

Arrange 20 gyoza wrappers on work surface. Spoon 1 rounded teaspoon filling into center of each. Brush edges with egg. Top each with another wrapper; press edges firmly to seal. Using 2¼-inch-diameter fluted cookie cutter, cut each ravioli into scalloped round. *(Ravioli can be prepared 8 hours ahead. Arrange in single layer on flour-dusted, plastic-lined baking sheets. Cover and refrigerate.)*

Cook butter in heavy medium saucepan over medium-high heat until butter begins to brown, about 3 minutes. Add 4 teaspoons sage, 1½ cups stock and ¼ cup wine and boil until reduced to ½ cup, about 12 minutes (butter will separate from sauce).

Meanwhile, cook ravioli in batches in large pot of boiling salted water until just tender but still firm to bite, about 5 minutes per batch. Using slotted spoon, transfer ravioli to shallow soup bowls. Whisk butter sauce and spoon over ravioli. Sprinkle with remaining 1 teaspoon sage and serve.

4 SERVINGS

Seafood Pizza

◆ ◆ ◆

12   mussels, scrubbed, debearded
½   cup dry white wine
14   sun-dried tomatoes (not packed in oil), chopped
4   large garlic cloves, minced
1   large shallot, minced

1   cup canned crushed tomatoes with added puree
½   teaspoon grated lemon peel
¼   teaspoon dried crushed red pepper

10   large uncooked shrimp, peeled, deveined, cut in half lengthwise
5   ounces bay scallops

1   12-inch-diameter baked cheese pizza crust (such as Boboli)
1   tablespoon Garlic Oil (see recipe on page 137)
¾   cup grated mozzarella cheese (about 3 ounces)
1   tablespoon minced fresh basil or 1 teaspoon dried
2   tablespoons freshly grated Parmesan cheese

Combine first 5 ingredients in heavy large skillet over medium-high heat. Cover; boil just until mussels open, shaking pan occasionally, about 4 minutes. Using tongs, transfer mussels to work surface, discarding any that do not open.

Add crushed tomatoes, lemon peel and dried red pepper to same skillet. Stir over medium-high heat until sauce is thick, about 4 minutes. Remove mussels from shells; discard shells and place mussels in small bowl. *(Mussels and sauce can be prepared 1 day ahead. Cover separately and refrigerate.)*

Preheat oven to 450°F. Bring sauce to simmer over medium-high heat. Add shrimp and scallops and cook until seafood is almost cooked through, about 3 minutes. Remove from heat. Cool 10 minutes. Stir in mussels. Season to taste with salt and pepper.

Place crust on large baking sheet. Brush with Garlic Oil. Bake crust until golden brown and edges begin to crisp, about 10 minutes. Stir mozzarella and basil into seafood mixture. Spoon over hot crust. Sprinkle with Parmesan cheese.

Bake pizza until shrimp and scallops are cooked through and mozzarella cheese melts, about 6 minutes. Transfer pizza to cutting board. Cool 5 minutes. Cut into wedges and serve.

MAKES 1 LARGE PIZZA

MEDITERRANEAN CHEESES

Throughout the Mediterranean, a wide variety of cheeses adds flavor and substance to traditional dishes.

In Italy, nutty-flavored Parmesan and the stronger Pecorino, made of sheep's milk, are eaten thinly sliced or grated over soups, casseroles and salads. Buffalo-milk mozzarella and ricotta are both essential ingredients in many Italian pastas and pizzas. France's fresh white *fromage blanc* is often used as a base in a variety of Mediterranean recipes.

In Greek cooking, versatile feta cheese lends its pleasantly salty taste to simple salads and phyllo-wrapped appetizers. *Manchego* cheese is to Spain what Parmesan is to Italy. Made from sheep's milk, it ranges from soft to hard in texture and from mild to pungent in flavor.

The Middle East has a version of ricotta, *gebna beyda*, in addition to *labni*, a popular cheese made from fresh yogurt that has been drained through cheesecloth. Israel's *labaneh* is a tangy, soft yogurt cheese that is often seasoned with sesame seeds, spices and olive oil. Goat cheeses are also popular throughout the region.

◆ ◆ ◆

Artichoke Pizza with Goat Cheese and Sausage

♦ ♦ ♦

½   pound sweet Italian sausage, casings removed

1   13.75- to 14-ounce can artichoke hearts, drained
⅓   cup roasted red bell peppers from jar, drained
20   brine-cured black olives (such as Kalamata), pitted
2   tablespoons chopped fresh basil or 2 teaspoons dried
1   cup grated mozzarella cheese (about 4 ounces)
⅓   cup freshly grated Parmesan cheese (about 1 ounce)

1   12-inch-diameter baked cheese pizza crust (such as Boboli)
1   tablespoon Garlic Oil (see recipe on page 137)
½   cup (generous) crumbled soft fresh goat cheese (such as Montrachet; about 2 ounces)

Sauté sausage in heavy medium skillet over medium heat until cooked through, crumbling sausage with spoon, about 10 minutes. Using slotted spoon, transfer to paper towels and drain.

Combine artichoke hearts, bell peppers, 12 olives and basil in processor. Using on/off turns, process until finely chopped. Transfer mixture to large bowl. Stir in sausage and mozzarella and Parmesan cheeses. *(Can be prepared 1 day ahead. Refrigerate.)*

Preheat oven to 450°F. Place crust on large baking sheet. Brush with Garlic Oil. Spread artichoke mixture over crust. Dot with goat cheese. Top with 8 olives. Season with pepper. Bake pizza until crust is golden and mozzarella bubbles, about 15 minutes. Transfer to cutting board. Cool 5 minutes. Cut into wedges.

MAKES 1 LARGE PIZZA

♦ ♦ ♦

PIZZA PARTY FOR TEN

SPINACH, GORGONZOLA AND PINE NUT PIZZA
(PAGE 137; PICTURED OPPOSITE)

FONTINA, PROSCIUTTO AND TOMATO PIZZA
(PAGE 136; PICTURED OPPOSITE)

ARTICHOKE PIZZA WITH GOAT CHEESE AND SAUSAGE
(AT LEFT; PICTURED OPPOSITE)

SEAFOOD PIZZA
(PAGE 133; PICTURED OPPOSITE)

THREE-GREENS SALAD
(PAGE 157)

TIRAMISÙ

♦ ♦ ♦

Fontina, Prosciutto and Tomato Pizza

◆ ◆ ◆

1   cup grated Fontina cheese (about 4 ounces)
1   cup shredded mozzarella cheese (about 4 ounces)
½   cup finely chopped prosciutto (about 2 ounces)
¼   cup chopped red onion
2   teaspoons minced fresh rosemary or ¾ teaspoon dried

1   12-inch-diameter baked cheese pizza crust (such as Boboli)
1   tablespoon Garlic Oil (see recipe on page 137)
10 plum tomatoes, halved crosswise, seeded, cut into thin rounds
2   tablespoons freshly grated Parmesan cheese (about ½ ounce)

Combine first 5 ingredients in bowl. Season generously with pepper. *(Can be made 1 day ahead. Cover and chill.)*

Preheat oven to 450°F. Place crust on heavy large baking sheet. Brush with Garlic Oil. Spoon cheese mixture over crust. Arrange overlapping tomatoes in concentric circles atop cheese mixture. Sprinkle with Parmesan cheese. Bake pizza until crust is golden brown and cheese bubbles, about 18 minutes. Transfer pizza to cutting board. Cool 5 minutes. Cut into wedges.

MAKES 1 LARGE PIZZA

Mini Pizzas

◆ ◆ ◆

24 slices firm white bread

¾   pound sweet or hot Italian sausages, casings removed
3   large garlic cloves, chopped
1   cup packed grated mozzarella cheese (about 4 ounces)
¾   cup purchased pizza or marinara sauce
⅓   cup freshly grated Parmesan cheese (about 1 ounce)

Preheat oven to 350°F. Lightly oil 24 muffin cups. Using 2½- to 2¾-inch-diameter cookie cutter, cut out center of each bread slice (reserve trimmings for another use). Press bread rounds onto bottoms and about ½ inch up sides of prepared cups, forming crusts.

Sauté sausage and garlic in heavy large skillet over medium heat until brown, breaking up sausage with spoon, about 15 minutes. Using slotted spoon, transfer mixture to bowl; mix in mozzarella, ½ cup

pizza sauce and Parmesan. Divide filling among crusts. Top each with ½ teaspoon of remaining sauce.

Bake pizzas until crusts are light brown and filling is heated through, about 20 minutes. Serve hot.

MAKES 24

Spinach, Gorgonzola and Pine Nut Pizza

◆ ◆ ◆

1   tablespoon olive oil
1   onion, sliced
2   garlic cloves, minced
1   10-ounce package frozen spinach leaves, thawed, drained well, squeezed dry

1   12-inch-diameter baked cheese pizza crust (such as Boboli)
1   tablespoon Garlic Oil (see recipe below)
4   ounces Gorgonzola cheese, crumbled
3   ounces grated mozzarella cheese
¼   cup pine nuts (about 1 ounce)

Heat oil in heavy large skillet over medium heat. Add onion and sauté until very tender and golden, about 10 minutes. Add garlic; sauté 2 minutes. Add spinach to skillet and cook until liquid evaporates, separating leaves with spoon, about 3 minutes. Cool.

Preheat oven to 450°F. Place crust on baking sheet. Brush crust with Garlic Oil. Top with spinach mixture. Sprinkle Gorgonzola and mozzarella over spinach. Top with nuts. Season with pepper.

Bake pizza until crust is golden brown and cheese bubbles, about 15 minutes. Transfer to cutting board. Cool 5 minutes.

MAKES 1 LARGE PIZZA

Garlic Oil

½   cup olive oil
6   large garlic cloves, pressed

Combine olive oil and garlic. Cover and refrigerate overnight. *(Can be made 2 days ahead; keep refrigerated.)* Let stand at room temperature 30 minutes before using.

MAKES ½ CUP

PIZZA PRIMER

The Greeks may get the credit for baking some form of the first pizza. But it's the Italians who turned this ingeniously simple meal-in-a-dish—in which the dish *is* the meal—into a higher art form. The Neapolitans introduced the first tomato-cheese classic; from that point forward, literally hundreds of other versions evolved throughout Italy, Sicily and on into southern France (where *pissaladière* developed a uniquely French flair and flavor).

In the United States, the pizzeria idea took off during the forties and fifties, followed shortly thereafter by the popularity of regional specialties, from the New York style, with its thin crust, to the hefty, deep-dish Chicago-style. By the eighties, California got into the picture with its own West Coast take on pizza pie.

These days, it's as easy to make pizza at home as it is to order one in. Packaged unbaked crusts, which you unroll, top and bake, and Bobolis, already-baked cheese pizza crusts, make quick work of the pizza's bottom half, leaving the cook plenty of time to ponder possible toppings.

◆ ◆ ◆

· On the Side ·

It is no coincidence that, when we've eaten a memorable meal, we'll often describe it as one that had "all the trimmings." Carefully chosen to complement a main course, the side dish — whether it's a vegetable, salad or bread, or any combination of the three — can elevate a good menu to exceptional status.

Take the selection of recipes in this chapter as examples of how a side dish can enhance any meal. Accompany a holiday roast with Baby Carrots with Tarragon (page 145) or Potato and Celery Root Puree (page 150), and the occasion becomes all the more special. Round out the family table with Spinach-Cheddar Casserole (page 146), and a weekday dinner rises above the ordinary. Dishes such as Sweet Couscous with Nuts and Dates (page 149) and Pinto Beans with Tortilla-Cheese Crust (page 144) contribute authentic ethnic flair to any menu. Planning a weekend barbecue? Pile the table high with Picnic Potato Salad (page 158) or Brown Rice, Corn and Grilled Vegetable Salad (page 155), and watch burgers-on-the-grill take on a whole new meaning.

And don't forget the baked goods. From Sage Focaccia (page 165) to Oat and Walnut Buttermilk Braid (page 162), Irish Wheat Bread (page 164) to Onion-Fennel Flatbreads (page 169), fresh-from-the-oven bread may be all the trimming you need to make a breakfast, brunch, lunch or dinner a meal to be reckoned with.

Tomato, Caper, Olive and Blue Cheese Salad, page 152.

White Beans with Tomatoes and Chilies

◆ ◆ ◆

1	tablespoon olive oil
2	tablespoons chopped drained canned pickled jalapeño chilies
1½	tablespoons chopped fresh sage or 2 teaspoons dried rubbed sage
1	tablespoon chopped garlic
2	15-ounce cans cannellini (white kidney beans), drained
1¾	cups canned crushed tomatoes with added puree

Heat olive oil in heavy medium saucepan over medium heat. Add jalapeño chilies, sage and chopped garlic and sauté until garlic is tender but not brown, about 5 minutes. Add cannellini beans and tomatoes and simmer until mixture thickens and flavors blend, about 15 minutes. Season to taste with salt and pepper and serve.

4 SERVINGS

Were you in Tuscany, this delicious side dish would be called *fagioli all'uccelletto*. To turn the beans into a light meatless meal, mix them with freshly cooked pasta.

◆ ◆ ◆

Baby Squash with Capers and Parsley

◆ ◆ ◆

4½	tablespoons olive oil
2	pounds whole baby squash (such as zucchini, crookneck and pattypan)
3	tablespoons water
6	tablespoons drained capers, minced
4½	tablespoons chopped fresh parsley
3	tablespoons fresh lemon juice

Heat oil in large skillet over medium-high heat. Add squash and water. Cover; cook squash until almost crisp-tender, about 4 minutes. Uncover; stir until liquid evaporates and squash is crisp-tender, about 2 minutes. Transfer to bowl.

Add capers, parsley and lemon juice to squash and toss to coat. Season with salt and pepper. Serve warm or at room temperature.

10 SERVINGS

Red Onion, Goat Cheese and Basil Tart

◆ ◆ ◆

2   medium-size red onions, unpeeled, each cut into 12 wedges
3   tablespoons olive oil

1   sheet frozen puff pastry (half of 17¼-ounce package), thawed
1   large egg, beaten to blend

8   ounces soft fresh goat cheese (such as Montrachet)
¼   cup purchased pesto
¼   cup whipping cream
3   tablespoons chopped fresh basil

Preheat oven to 400°F. Oil heavy large baking sheet. Toss onion wedges with oil in medium bowl. Season with salt and pepper. Arrange onions in single layer on baking sheet. Bake until bottoms of onions are golden and onions are very tender, about 25 minutes. Transfer sheet to rack; cool. *(Can be made 1 day ahead. Cover and let stand at room temperature.)*

Preheat oven to 400°F. Roll out pastry on lightly floured surface to 14 x 11-inch rectangle. Trim edges to even. Cut ½-inch strip from each side of pastry, forming 13 x 10-inch rectangle; reserve strips. Transfer pastry rectangle to another heavy large baking sheet. Brush edges with some of beaten egg; reserve remaining egg. Place strips on edges of tart, creating border. Trim strips; press gently to adhere. Pierce bottom of pastry several times with fork. Bake until edges puff and pastry is golden brown, about 15 minutes. Transfer baking sheet to rack. Using metal spatula, loosen pastry from baking sheet. Cool on sheet. Reduce oven temperature to 350°F.

Stir cheese, pesto, cream and 2 tablespoons basil in medium bowl until smooth. Season with salt and pepper. Mix in remaining beaten egg. Spread cheese mixture evenly over bottom of crust. Remove peel and stem end from roasted onions. Fan wedges, golden brown side up, over cheese mixture.

Bake tart until crust is brown and cheese appears set, about 20 minutes. Transfer sheet to rack; cool tart to room temperature. Sprinkle tart with remaining basil. Cut into squares.

10 SERVINGS

SETTING THE SCENE

The versatile side dish at left is featured in the Garden Party menu on page 83.
The tart is cut into squares, making it especially easy to eat — something to think about when you're planning a buffet. In addition to the menu, planning should include the setting, too. Here are some ideas.

◆ One or two baskets of fresh fruits and vegetables would make a charming centerpiece. For something even more rustic, arrange the produce in a wooden crate that has a colorful fruit label.

◆ Make a garland of greenery from ivy, bougainvillea and lemon leaves, and swag it along the edge of the table. Or shape it into an "S" down the center of the table.

◆ Use twists of ivy to make individual napkin rings.

◆ For candles, try the casual, thick, squat type, called pillars. Set them on a plate or in a shallow bowl, and surround them with a wreath of herbs or small flowers.

◆ Fill a big bucket with ice to keep drinks cold, and add some jasmine or orange and lemon blossoms to the ice to perfume the air.

◆ ◆ ◆

Artichokes with Lemon and Dill

◆ ◆ ◆

2 tablespoons plus ¼ cup fresh lemon juice
6 fresh artichokes (about 3¾ pounds)
1 lemon, halved

⅓ cup olive oil
8 green onions, chopped (about 2 cups)
3 cups (or more) water
¼ cup chopped fresh dill
2 teaspoons sugar
1½ teaspoons salt

2 tablespoons all purpose flour

Pour 2 tablespoons lemon juice into large bowl of water. Cut stem from 1 artichoke; pull off and discard 3 outer bottom layers of leaves, exposing pale green base. Carefully trim artichoke base and leaf ends. Cut artichoke in half. Using small spoon, remove choke and prickly leaves from center. Rub cut edges of artichoke with cut side of lemon half. Place artichoke in bowl of water and lemon juice. Repeat with remaining artichokes.

Heat oil in large Dutch oven over medium-high heat. Add green onions; sauté until tender, about 3 minutes. Add 3 cups water, dill, sugar, salt and ¼ cup lemon juice. Bring to simmer. Drain artichokes; add to Dutch oven. Cover; simmer until artichoke bottoms are tender and leaves can be pulled off easily, occasionally pushing artichokes under water, about 30 minutes. Using slotted spoon, transfer artichokes to platter; reserve cooking liquid. Tent artichokes with foil to keep warm, or let cool to room temperature.

Place flour in small bowl. Whisk in ½ cup cooking liquid. Pour flour mixture into liquid in Dutch oven; bring to boil, stirring. Cook until sauce thickens, stirring constantly and thinning with more water if necessary, about 2 minutes. Season with salt and pepper. Pour over artichokes. Serve warm or at room temperature.

4 SERVINGS

Grilled Tomatoes with Aioli

◆ ◆ ◆

⅓ cup mayonnaise
1 large garlic clove, pressed
¾ teaspoon fresh lemon juice

2 large tomatoes (about 1½ pounds), cut crosswise in half
1½ tablespoons olive oil

Whisk mayonnaise, garlic and lemon juice in bowl to blend.
Prepare barbecue (medium-high heat). When coals turn white, drain chips, if using, and scatter over coals. When chips begin to smoke, brush cut side of tomatoes with oil and place on grill, cut side down. Cover and grill tomatoes until hot, juicy and tender, about 3 minutes per side. Transfer to plate. Season tomatoes with salt and pepper. Top each tomato half with dollop of garlic mayonnaise.

4 SERVINGS

◆ ◆ ◆

The fire's smoky heat — and some luscious aioli (that garlicky mayonnaise so popular in Southern France) — turn simple grilled tomatoes into a spectacular side dish.

◆ ◆ ◆

Corn on the Cob with Shallot-Thyme Butter

◆ ◆ ◆

8 tablespoons (1 stick) butter, room temperature
⅔ cup chopped shallots (about 3 ounces)
2 tablespoons chopped fresh thyme or 2 teaspoons dried

6 to 9 ears fresh corn, shucked
   Olive oil

Melt 2 tablespoons butter in heavy small skillet over medium heat. Add shallots and sauté until brown, about 4 minutes. Cool. Combine remaining 6 tablespoons butter and thyme in small bowl. Add shallot mixture and blend well. Season with salt and pepper.

Prepare barbecue (medium-high heat). Brush corn with olive oil. Grill corn away from direct heat until just cooked and beginning to brown in a few places, turning frequently, about 10 minutes. Alternatively, omit brushing corn with olive oil and cook in large pot of boiling salted water until tender, about 6 minutes; drain. Serve corn immediately with shallot-thyme butter.

6 SERVINGS

Pinto Beans with Tortilla-Cheese Crust

◆ ◆ ◆

This bean "casserole," with its cheesy, tortilla-chip topping, is a great side dish when the main course is a simply cooked meat dish. We suggest it with the ribs on page 68, but it would also be good with grilled steaks or barbecued chicken.

◆ ◆ ◆

4	15-ounce cans pinto beans, rinsed, drained
2	tablespoons vegetable oil
2	cups chopped onions
1	cup chopped red bell pepper
1	cup chopped yellow bell pepper
2	tablespoons chopped garlic
2	tablespoons chili powder
2	teaspoons ground cumin
1	28-ounce can Italian-style tomatoes, drained, chopped, juices reserved
1	cup canned chicken broth
1	teaspoon hot pepper sauce (such as Tabasco)
8	tablespoons chopped fresh cilantro
¾	cup finely crushed tortilla chips
1	cup packed grated Monterey Jack cheese with jalapeños

Puree 1 can beans in processor. Heat oil in Dutch oven over medium heat. Add onions and bell peppers; sauté until soft, about 10 minutes. Add garlic; sauté 2 minutes. Add chili powder and cumin; stir 1 minute. Mix in tomatoes, ½ cup juices, broth, pepper sauce, whole beans and pureed beans. Simmer mixture 5 minutes, stirring often. Add 6 tablespoons cilantro. Season with salt and pepper. Pour into 13 x 9 x 2-inch glass baking dish. *(Can be made 1 day ahead. Cover and refrigerate.)*

Preheat oven to 400°F. Sprinkle crushed chips over beans. Bake until heated through, about 30 minutes. Top with cheese; bake until melted, about 5 minutes. Top with 2 tablespoons cilantro.

8 SERVINGS

Creamed Spinach with Chèvre

◆ ◆ ◆

3   10-ounce packages ready-to-use spinach leaves

½   cup whipping cream
2   ounces soft fresh goat cheese (such as Montrachet)
1   large shallot, minced
½   teaspoon grated lemon peel

Preheat oven to 250°F. Bring 2 inches of water to boil in large pot. Add spinach and cook just until wilted, constantly pressing spinach down into water, about 2 minutes. Transfer ½ cup cooking liquid to medium skillet and reserve. Drain spinach in colander, firmly pressing out excess water. Transfer spinach to ovenproof platter. Place in oven to keep warm.

Add cream, goat cheese, shallot and lemon peel to cooking liquid in skillet. Stir over medium-high heat until sauce is thick and reduced to ⅔ cup, about 6 minutes. Season with salt and pepper.

Pour sauce evenly over spinach. Serve immediately.

4 SERVINGS

Baby Carrots with Tarragon

◆ ◆ ◆

4   bunches baby carrots (each about 8 ounces), peeled, trimmed, 3 inches of stems left intact
¼   cup water
3   tablespoons minced fresh tarragon or 3 teaspoons dried
2   tablespoons (¼ stick) butter
1   tablespoon white wine vinegar
1   tablespoon honey

Combine carrots, ¼ cup water, 1½ tablespoons tarragon, butter, vinegar and honey in heavy large skillet. Bring to boil. Reduce heat to medium; cover and simmer until carrots are almost tender, about 12 minutes. Uncover; cook until carrots are tender and liquid is reduced to glaze, about 6 minutes longer. Season with salt and pepper. Transfer to platter. Sprinkle with 1½ tablespoons tarragon.

6 SERVINGS

◆ ◆ ◆

These days, goat cheese comes any number of ways — flavored, plain, wrapped with grape leaves or covered in ash. Find the one that appeals to your taste, then discover the special flavor it adds to salads, pastas, pizzas — even a classic dish like the delicious creamed spinach here.

"Drowned" Broccoli

◆ ◆ ◆

2 pounds broccoli
½ cup olive oil
2 large white onions, thinly sliced
6 tablespoons chopped fresh parsley
4 ounces caciocavallo or sharp provolone cheese (about ¾ cup), finely diced
16 brine-cured black olives (such as Kalamata), pitted, coarsely chopped
10 anchovy fillets, chopped
¾ cup dry red wine

Cut stalks from broccoli. Peel stalks, cut into 3-inch segments and thinly slice lengthwise. Separate broccoli crowns into florets. Heat olive oil in heavy large Dutch oven over medium-high heat. Add broccoli stalks and florets, sliced onions and chopped fresh parsley and sauté until onions are tender, about 10 minutes. Mix in cheese, chopped olives and anchovy fillets. Stir mixture 2 minutes. Add dry red wine and stir mixture to blend well. Reduce heat to low, cover Dutch oven and simmer 45 minutes.

Uncover Dutch oven and cook broccoli until very tender and wine evaporates, about 15 minutes longer. Season broccoli to taste with salt and pepper and serve.

6 SERVINGS

◆ ◆ ◆

In this Italian side dish, the broccoli is "drowned" in a heady mixture of olive oil, onions, anchovies, olives, red wine and cheese. While there are variations of this basic preparation throughout Italy, food historians generally think it to be of Sicilian origin.

◆ ◆ ◆

Spinach-Cheddar Casserole

◆ ◆ ◆

4 eggs
¾ teaspoon salt
½ teaspoon pepper
1 10-ounce package frozen chopped spinach, thawed, squeezed dry
1 16-ounce container cottage cheese
1 bunch green onions, chopped
1 cup packed grated sharp cheddar cheese
¼ cup all purpose flour
3 tablespoons chopped fresh dill or 1 tablespoon dillweed

Preheat oven to 350°F. Butter 8 x 8 x 2-inch glass baking dish. Beat eggs, salt and pepper to blend in large bowl. Mix in spinach. Add remaining ingredients and stir until well blended. Transfer mixture to prepared dish. Bake casserole until center is firm and top is golden, about 45 minutes. Serve immediately.

8 TO 10 SERVINGS

Spicy Black Beans with Bell Peppers and Rice

◆ ◆ ◆

1	tablespoon vegetable oil
1	large onion, diced
1	cup chopped green bell pepper
1	cup chopped red bell pepper
3	large garlic cloves, chopped
1	tablespoon ground cumin
1	jalapeño chili, seeded, chopped
1	teaspoon dried oregano
2	15- to 16-ounce cans black beans, drained
2	cups canned crushed tomatoes with added puree
¼	cup orange juice
1½	teaspoons hot pepper sauce (such as Tabasco)

| 1⅓ | cups rice, cooked |

Heat oil in heavy large skillet over medium-high heat. Add onion, bell peppers, garlic, cumin, jalapeño and oregano; sauté until vegetables begin to soften, about 8 minutes. Mash ½ cup beans. Add mashed beans, whole beans, tomatoes, orange juice and hot pepper sauce to skillet. Bring to boil, stirring frequently. Reduce heat, cover and simmer 15 minutes. Uncover and simmer until reduced to thick sauce consistency, stirring occasionally, about 15 minutes. Season with salt and pepper.

Mound rice in center of platter. Spoon black bean mixture over.

8 SERVINGS

◆ ◆ ◆

A quick and spicy — thanks to chopped jalapeños and hot pepper sauce — take on that southern classic, rice and beans. Served in larger portions, the dish would work as a meatless main course.

◆ ◆ ◆

Sautéed Baby Vegetables

◆ ◆ ◆

24 baby carrots, peeled

½ cup (1 stick) butter
1 pound baby zucchini, trimmed
1 pound baby pattypan squash, trimmed
1 pound baby yellow crookneck or yellow zucchini squash, trimmed

Blanch carrots in large pot of boiling salted water 2 minutes. Drain; rinse with cold water. Drain well.

Divide butter between 2 heavy large skillets; melt over medium-high heat. Add half of carrots and remaining vegetables to each skillet. Sauté until crisp tender and beginning to brown in spots, tossing occasionally, about 10 minutes. Season to taste with salt and pepper. Transfer vegetables to large bowl.

12 SERVINGS

Ratatouille with Fresh Basil

◆ ◆ ◆

1 small eggplant (about 1 pound), cut into ¾-inch cubes

8 tablespoons olive oil
2 large red bell peppers, cut into ¾-inch pieces
1 large onion, coarsely chopped
12 ounces small zucchini, cut into ¾-inch-thick rounds

1 pound tomatoes, peeled, seeded, coarsely chopped
4 garlic cloves, chopped
1 tablespoon chopped fresh thyme or 1 teaspoon dried
1 bay leaf
2 teaspoons red wine vinegar (optional)
⅓ cup chopped fresh basil

Place eggplant in colander. Sprinkle with salt. Let stand 30 minutes. Pat eggplant dry with paper towels.

Heat 4 tablespoons olive oil in heavy large nonstick skillet over medium-high heat. Add eggplant and sauté until brown and cooked through, about 6 minutes. Transfer eggplant to large bowl. Heat 1 tablespoon olive oil in same skillet over medium-high heat. Add bell peppers and sauté until light brown, about 5 minutes. Add bell peppers to eggplant. Add 1 tablespoon olive oil to same skillet. Add chopped onion and sauté until light brown, about 4 minutes. Add onion to eggplant. Heat 1 tablespoon olive oil in same skillet over medium-high heat. Add sliced zucchini and brown lightly, about 3 minutes. Add to vegetables in bowl.

Heat 1 tablespoon olive oil in same skillet. Add tomatoes, garlic, thyme and bay leaf and sauté mixture 3 minutes. Return all vegetables to skillet. Reduce heat to medium, cover and cook until vegetables are very tender, stirring occasionally, about 20 minutes. Season ratatouille to taste with salt and pepper. Mix in 2 teaspoons red wine vinegar, if desired. Discard bay leaf. Mix basil into ratatouille.

6 SERVINGS

Sweet Couscous with Nuts and Dates

◆ ◆ ◆

2⅔ cups couscous (about 1 pound)

2⅔ cups water

½ cup sugar

¼ cup vegetable oil

1½ cups chopped toasted mixed nuts (such as walnuts, blanched almonds, hazelnuts, pistachios and pine nuts)

1 8-ounce box pitted dates, cut into pieces

2 cups milk, hot
 Additional sugar

Place couscous in large bowl. Bring 2⅔ cups water, ½ cup sugar and oil to boil in heavy large saucepan, stirring to dissolve sugar. Pour mixture over couscous and stir until well blended. Cover and let stand 10 minutes. Fluff with fork to separate grains. Mix in nuts and dates. Transfer couscous to 13 x 9 x 2-inch baking dish. Cool completely. Cover with foil. *(Couscous can be prepared 4 hours ahead. Let stand at room temperature until ready to bake.)*

Preheat oven to 350°F. Bake couscous until heated through, about 20 minutes. Spoon into bowls. Serve couscous, passing hot milk and additional sugar separately.

8 SERVINGS

◆ ◆ ◆

In this interesting specialty from Tunisia called *farka*, the semolina grains take a sweet turn. It is enjoyed as a side dish, breakfast dish or afternoon snack rather than an after-dinner dessert. For another Tunisian specialty, turn to the Aromatic Fish Soup with Potatoes on page 32.

◆ ◆ ◆

Potato and Celery Root Puree

◆ ◆ ◆

Mashed potatoes — done a little differently. This side dish goes especially well with the pork tenderloin on page 66. If you plan on preparing it the day before serving, reserve ¼ cup of the cooking liquid and add it to the puree when reheating it.

◆ ◆ ◆

1   1¼-pound celery root (celeriac), peeled, cut into 1-inch pieces
1¼   pounds russet potatoes, peeled, cut into 1-inch pieces
     Salt
¼   cup whipping cream
2   tablespoons (¼ stick) butter
     Celery salt

Place celery root and potatoes in large saucepan. Cover with water; salt lightly. Boil until very tender, about 15 minutes. Drain vegetables, reserving ¼ cup liquid. Return vegetables to same saucepan. Add cream and butter and mash until almost smooth. Season with celery salt and pepper. *(Can be prepared 1 day ahead. Cover puree and cooking liquid separately and refrigerate. Stir puree over medium heat until heated through, adding reserved cooking liquid if mixture is dry.)*

4 SERVINGS

Barley, Corn, Red Pepper and Green Onion Pilaf

◆ ◆ ◆

Grains are great — nutritious, versatile, delicious and just right for the way we eat today. Barley, an ancient grain with a newfound popularity, stars in this easy side dish.

◆ ◆ ◆

1   tablespoon olive oil
1   large red bell pepper, chopped
2   bunches green onions, chopped
1½   cups pearl barley
2   14½-ounce cans vegetable broth or chicken broth
2   cups frozen corn
½   cup sliced fresh basil

Heat oil in heavy medium saucepan over medium-high heat. Add chopped bell pepper and half of green onions and sauté until tender, about 5 minutes. Add barley and stir to coat with olive oil. Add vegetable broth and bring to boil, stirring occasionally. Reduce heat, cover and simmer until barley is tender, stirring occasionally, about 40 minutes. Add corn and stir until heated through, about 5 minutes. Mix in sliced basil and remaining green onions. Season to taste with salt and pepper and serve.

6 SERVINGS

New Potatoes with Basil

◆ ◆ ◆

1½ pounds small red-skinned potatoes (about 1 to 1½ inches in diameter)
2   tablespoons (¼ stick) butter
4   tablespoons finely chopped fresh basil
2   large shallots, minced
2   large garlic cloves, minced

Pierce potatoes in several places with fork. Melt butter in heavy large skillet over medium heat. Add potatoes and season with salt and pepper. Cover and cook until potatoes are almost tender, shaking skillet occasionally, about 25 minutes. Add 2 tablespoons basil, shallots and garlic. Reduce heat to medium-low; cover and cook until potatoes are golden brown and very tender, shaking skillet occasionally, about 10 minutes longer. Season with salt and pepper. Transfer to bowl. Sprinkle with remaining 2 tablespoons basil.

6 SERVINGS

Spicy Bacon, Onion and Cheese Potatoes

◆ ◆ ◆

8   slices bacon, coarsely chopped
2   pounds russet potatoes, peeled, cut into ½-inch pieces
1   large onion, chopped
1   cup packed grated hot pepper Monterey Jack cheese
2   tablespoons (¼ stick) butter

Preheat oven to 350°F. Butter 13 x 9 x 2-inch glass baking dish. Cook chopped bacon in heavy large skillet over medium heat until brown and crisp. Using slotted spoon, transfer bacon to paper towels and drain. Combine bacon, potatoes and onion in prepared baking dish. Season with salt and pepper. Sprinkle Monterey Jack cheese over and dot with butter. Cover with aluminum foil. Bake until potatoes and onions are very tender, about 1 hour.

Preheat broiler. Uncover baking dish and broil until top of potato mixture is brown and crisp, about 2 minutes.

8 SERVINGS

◆ ◆ ◆

This recipe comes straight from the files of a reader's family favorites. Quick to assemble, it bakes for an hour then gets a quick broiling to brown. Try it with broiled meats.

◆ ◆ ◆

This unique salad accompanies a tasty main course pasta dish in the Pacific Northwest menu on page 126. As you might have guessed, beets, sugar snap peas, arugula and dill are all crops that grow in abundance in the state of Washington.

Roasted Beet and Sugar Snap Pea Salad

◆ ◆ ◆

3   medium beets, trimmed

½   pound sugar snap peas, trimmed

1   tablespoon plus 1 teaspoon Dijon mustard
1   tablespoon plus 1 teaspoon cider vinegar
¼   cup olive oil
3   tablespoons chopped fresh dill or 1 tablespoon dillweed
1½   teaspoons sugar

2   ⅔-ounce packages fresh arugula, trimmed

Preheat oven to 375°F. Wrap beets in aluminum foil. Bake until tender, about 1 hour 15 minutes. Cool. Peel beets; cut into wedges.

Cook sugar snap peas in large saucepan of boiling salted water until crisp-tender, about 1 minute. Drain. Rinse with cold water; drain well. Pat sugar snap peas dry.

Mix mustard and vinegar in small bowl. Gradually mix in oil, then dill and sugar. *(Can be prepared 4 hours ahead. Cover sugar snap peas and refrigerate. Cover dressing and beets separately and let stand at room temperature.)*

Line platter with arugula. Mix beets, peas and dressing in medium bowl. Season with salt and pepper. Spoon atop arugula.

4 SERVINGS

Tomato, Caper, Olive and Blue Cheese Salad

◆ ◆ ◆

6   large tomatoes, sliced
2   tablespoons balsamic vinegar
5   tablespoons olive oil
⅓   cup halved pitted brine-cured black olives (such as Kalamata)

⅓ cup crumbled blue cheese (about 2 ounces)
2 tablespoons drained capers
4 anchovies, drained, chopped (optional)
　 Fresh basil leaves

Arrange tomatoes on large platter. Drizzle with vinegar, then oil. Sprinkle very lightly with salt and generously with pepper. Sprinkle with olives, blue cheese, capers and anchovies, if desired. Garnish with basil leaves and serve.

6 SERVINGS

Green Bean and Red Onion Salad with Radish Dressing

◆ ◆ ◆

5 radishes, unpeeled, trimmed, coarsely chopped
½ cup olive oil
2 tablespoons Sherry wine vinegar
1 tablespoon honey mustard
½ teaspoon minced garlic

1½ pounds slender green beans, trimmed

4 cups mixed greens (such as red leaf lettuce and baby spinach), torn into bite-size pieces
1 red onion, thinly sliced
2 large radishes, sliced paper-thin (optional)

◆ ◆ ◆

Radishes add their distinctive, peppery taste to the dressing for this light and refreshing salad. It makes a fine partner for the pot pies on page 70.

◆ ◆ ◆

Place 5 radishes in processor. Add oil, vinegar, mustard and garlic; process until thick dressing forms. Season with salt and pepper. Transfer to small bowl. *(Can be made 1 day ahead. Cover; chill. Bring just to room temperature before using.)*

Cook green beans in large pot of boiling salted water until just crisp-tender, about 5 minutes. Drain beans and rinse under cold water. Drain. Pat dry with paper towels. Wrap in kitchen towels and place in plastic bag. Chill until cold, at least 1 hour and up to 1 day.

Place beans, mixed greens and onion in large bowl. Toss with enough dressing to coat. Season with salt and pepper. Garnish with sliced radishes, if desired. Serve immediately.

8 SERVINGS

Papaya Salad with Asparagus and Fennel

◆ ◆ ◆

DRESSING

½   cup papaya nectar

¼   cup chopped macadamia nuts
¼   cup vegetable oil
2   tablespoons finely chopped shallot
1   tablespoon fresh lemon juice

SALAD

2   tablespoons olive oil
1   garlic clove, pressed
1   pound fresh asparagus, trimmed
1   fennel bulb, cut vertically into ¼-inch-thick slices

1   papaya, peeled, seeded, sliced
1   avocado, peeled, pitted, sliced

FOR DRESSING: Boil nectar in heavy small saucepan over high heat until reduced to ¼ cup, about 6 minutes. Cool.

Whisk nectar, nuts, vegetable oil, shallot and lemon juice in small bowl to blend. Season with salt and pepper.

FOR SALAD: Prepare barbecue (medium-high heat) or preheat broiler. Mix olive oil and garlic in bowl. Drizzle over asparagus and

fennel. Season with salt and pepper. Grill asparagus and fennel until slightly charred, about 4 minutes per side. Transfer to plate.

Arrange papaya and avocado slices on 4 plates. Top with asparagus and fennel. Drizzle with dressing.

4 SERVINGS

Brown Rice, Corn and Grilled Vegetable Salad

◆ ◆ ◆

1½ cups brown rice

4 zucchini, halved lengthwise
1 large red onion, cut crosswise into 3 thick slices
¼ cup plus ⅓ cup olive oil
5 tablespoons soy sauce
3 tablespoons Worcestershire sauce

1½ cups mesquite wood chips, soaked in cold water 1 hour (optional)
2 cups fresh corn kernels

⅔ cup fresh orange juice
1 tablespoon fresh lemon juice
½ cup chopped Italian parsley

Add rice to large pot of boiling salted water. Cover partially and cook until just tender, about 30 minutes. Drain well. Transfer to large bowl and cool to room temperature, stirring occasionally.

Place zucchini and onion slices in shallow dish. Mix ¼ cup oil, 2 tablespoons soy sauce and 2 tablespoons Worcestershire sauce in small bowl. Pour over vegetables. Let stand 30 minutes, turning once.

Prepare barbecue (medium-high heat). When coals turn white, drain chips, if using, and scatter over coals. When chips begin to smoke, season onion and zucchini with salt and pepper and place on grill. Cover and cook until tender and brown, occasionally turning and basting with marinade, about 8 minutes. Transfer to platter. Cut onion slices into quarters. Cut zucchini crosswise into 1-inch pieces. Add onion and zucchini to rice. Mix in corn.

Whisk orange juice, lemon juice, ⅓ cup oil, 3 tablespoons soy sauce and 1 tablespoon Worcestershire sauce in medium bowl. Pour 1 cup dressing over salad and toss to coat. Stir in parsley. Season with salt and pepper. Serve salad, passing remaining dressing.

6 SERVINGS

◆ ◆ ◆

Here, smoky vegetables, corn and brown rice are dressed with a citrus vinaigrette. This salad goes well with the meatless burgers on page 111.

◆ ◆ ◆

Tomato, Basil and Couscous Salad

◆ ◆ ◆

2¼ cups canned chicken broth
1   10-ounce box couscous

1   cup chopped green onions
1   cup (generous) diced seeded plum tomatoes
⅓   cup thinly sliced fresh basil
½   cup olive oil
¼   cup balsamic vinegar
¼   teaspoon dried crushed red pepper
    Cherry tomatoes, halved

Bring broth to boil in medium saucepan. Add couscous. Remove from heat. Cover; let stand 5 minutes. Transfer to large bowl. Fluff couscous with fork. Cool completely.

Mix all ingredients except cherry tomatoes into couscous. Season with salt and pepper. *(Can be made 1 day ahead. Chill.)* Garnish with cherry tomatoes and serve.

6 SERVINGS

◆ ◆ ◆

This simple salad is perfect picnic fare. It travels well and does not have any lettuce that might wilt and look unappealing. Transport it in an air-tight container, then transfer it to a pretty bowl and garnish with cherry tomatoes before serving.

◆ ◆ ◆

Cucumber, Olive, Radish, Arugula and Feta Salad

◆ ◆ ◆

1   English hothouse cucumber, quartered lengthwise, cut crosswise into ½-inch-wide pieces
1   bunch radishes, quartered
½   pound brine-cured black olives (such as Kalamata)
1   bunch (½ ounce) arugula, chopped
2   tablespoons olive oil
1   tablespoon fresh lemon juice
⅓   pound feta cheese, cubed

Combine cucumber, radishes, olives and arugula in medium bowl. *(Can be prepared 6 hours ahead. Cover and refrigerate.)* Add oil and lemon juice; toss to coat. Season to taste with salt and pepper. Mix in feta cheese. Serve immediately.

6 SERVINGS

Three-Greens Salad

◆ ◆ ◆

2   tablespoons fresh lemon juice
1   tablespoon balsamic vinegar
2   teaspoons Dijon mustard
2   teaspoons anchovy paste
1   large garlic clove, pressed
1   teaspoon Worcestershire sauce
⅓   cup olive oil

1   large head romaine lettuce, torn into bite-size pieces
1   large head radicchio, torn into bite-size pieces
3   bunches arugula, stemmed, torn into bite-size pieces

Combine first 6 ingredients in medium bowl. Gradually whisk in oil. Season generously with pepper. *(Can be made 2 days ahead. Chill. Let stand at room temperature 30 minutes before using.)*
Combine romaine, radicchio and arugula in large bowl. Rewhisk dressing to blend. Toss salad with enough dressing to coat.

10 TO 12 SERVINGS

◆ ◆ ◆

Five distinctive Mediterranean ingredients harmonize beautifully in this takeoff on the classic Greek salad. Offer wedges of pita bread alongside.

Picnic Potato Salad

◆ ◆ ◆

3½ pounds red-skinned potatoes, peeled, cut into ¾-inch pieces
3 tablespoons white wine vinegar

2 hard-boiled eggs, chopped
½ cup chopped onion
½ cup chopped celery
⅓ cup chopped Italian parsley
¾ cup mayonnaise
¾ cup sour cream
4 teaspoons Dijon mustard

Cook potatoes in large pot of boiling salted water just until tender, about 12 minutes. Drain. Transfer potatoes to large bowl. Drizzle vinegar over hot potatoes. Cool to room temperature.

Mix eggs, onion, celery and parsley into potatoes. Whisk mayonnaise, sour cream and mustard in medium bowl. Mix into potato mixture. Season salad with salt and pepper. *(Can be prepared 1 day ahead. Cover and refrigerate.)*

6 SERVINGS

◆ ◆ ◆

This is the kind of potato salad that purists dream of — plenty of tangy dressing and just a bit of crunch. Low-fat or nonfat mayonnaise and sour cream can be used if you're feeling virtuous.

◆ ◆ ◆

Sesame Soba Noodle and Vegetable Salad

◆ ◆ ◆

2 tablespoons sesame seeds

12 ounces dried buckwheat noodles (fancy soba)*
4 tablespoons peanut oil
1 tablespoon oriental sesame oil
6 tablespoons seasoned rice vinegar*
12 ounces English hothouse cucumber, seeded, shredded
8 ounces carrots, peeled, shredded
6 large radishes, trimmed, sliced
3 green onions, thinly sliced

Toast sesame seeds in heavy small skillet over medium-low heat. Cool sesame seeds completely.

Cook noodles in pot of boiling salted water until just tender but still firm to bite, about 8 minutes. Drain. Rinse noodles under cold water until cool. Drain well; transfer to large bowl. Add both oils and toss to coat. Mix vinegar and all remaining ingredients into noodles. Season with salt and pepper. Sprinkle with sesame seeds and serve.

Buckwheat noodles and seasoned rice vinegar are available at Asian markets and in the Asian section of some supermarkets.

6 SERVINGS

Pear Salad with Warm Shallot Dressing

◆ ◆ ◆

⅓   cup vegetable oil
3   large shallots, chopped
¼   cup fresh lemon juice
3   tablespoons canned vegetable broth

1   head butter lettuce, torn into bite-size pieces
1   large bunch watercress, trimmed
2   ripe but firm pears, cored, sliced
½   cup chopped walnuts, toasted
½   cup crumbled Gorgonzola cheese

Heat oil in heavy medium saucepan over medium-low heat. Add shallots and sauté until translucent, about 4 minutes. Mix in lemon juice and broth. Season to taste with salt and pepper.

Toss lettuce, watercress and warm dressing in large bowl. Divide greens among 6 plates. Arrange pear slices in spoke pattern on greens, dividing equally. Sprinkle with walnuts and cheese.

6 SERVINGS

ASIAN PASTA

Throughout Asia, pasta is served in a variety of forms and with every kind of meal, from a simple breakfast soup to a banquet finale of noodles to bless diners with longevity. The popularity of these unique pastas has spread to this side of the world, so much so that many kinds—in both dried and fresh forms—are available in supermarkets.

Asian noodles are generally made of wheat flour—with or without egg—or from rice flour, and come in a variety of lengths and shapes. Choose a noodle for its texture and flavor, as you would an Italian pasta.

Japanese buckwheat *soba* noodles, with their hearty flavor and texture, and bland, delicate Chinese cellophane noodles are two of the more common Asian pastas, but the variety of noodles available can be dizzying. As a rule of thumb, keep in mind the following: fresh wheat noodles in Mandarin China are called *sun mian* (*dan mian* are egg noodles); *udon* and *ramen* in Japan; *mee* in Thailand; and *panci mikit* in the Philippines. Fresh rice pastas, which are most popular in Southeast Asia and southern China, are called *fun* in Chinese and *kway teow* in Southeast Asia.

◆ ◆ ◆

Eggplant Salad with Miso Ginger Dressing

◆ ◆ ◆

⅓   cup rice vinegar

1   tablespoon miso*

1   tablespoon chopped fresh basil

2   teaspoons minced fresh ginger

1   large garlic clove, minced

¼   teaspoon dried crushed red pepper

⅔   cup vegetable oil

2   large Japanese eggplants, each cut lengthwise into 6 slices

1   tablespoon olive oil

8   cups mixed baby greens

Whisk first 6 ingredients in medium mixing bowl to blend. Gradually whisk in vegetable oil. Season with salt and pepper.

Prepare barbecue (medium-high heat) or preheat broiler. Brush eggplant with olive oil. Season with salt and pepper. Grill or broil until golden and just tender, about 3 minutes per side.

Toss greens with enough dressing to coat. Divide among plates. Top with eggplant. Drizzle with remaining dressing.

Fermented soybean paste is available at Asian markets, specialty foods stores and some supermarkets.

4 SERVINGS

Two-Bean and Roasted Red Pepper Salad

◆ ◆ ◆

8   ounces (about 1⅓ cups) dried Great Northern beans

2   teaspoons salt

1   large red bell pepper

8   ounces green beans, trimmed, cut crosswise into thirds
1   lemon

½   cup brine-cured black olives (such as Kalamata)
¼   cup olive oil
2   tablespoons red wine vinegar
1   tablespoon balsamic vinegar

Place dried beans in medium saucepan. Pour enough cold water over to cover beans by 3 inches. Let stand overnight.

Drain beans and return to same saucepan. Pour enough cold water over to cover beans by 3 inches. Bring to boil. Reduce heat; cover partially and simmer until tender, about 40 minutes. Add 2 teaspoons salt to beans and cool 15 minutes. Drain and cool beans.

Char bell pepper over gas flame or under broiler until blackened on all sides. Wrap in paper bag and let stand 10 minutes. Peel and seed pepper. Cut pepper into matchstick-size strips.

Cook green beans in pot of boiling salted water just until tender, about 4 minutes. Drain beans; transfer to bowl of ice water and cool. Drain. Using vegetable peeler, remove peel from lemon in long strips. Cut into very thin strips.

Combine Great Northern beans, bell pepper, green beans, lemon peel and olives in large bowl. Mix in oil and both vinegars. Season with salt and pepper and serve.

4 SERVINGS

◆ ◆ ◆

The two beans in this colorful salad are Great Northern and green beans. Strips of roasted red pepper and Kalamata olives add interest. Try this salad with the Grilled Rosemary Lamb Chops on page 61.

◆ ◆ ◆

◆ BREADS ◆

Oat and Walnut Buttermilk Braid

◆ ◆ ◆

½   cup warm water (105°F to 115°F)

¼   cup honey

1   envelope dry yeast

2   cups buttermilk

4⅓   cups (about) bread flour

2   cups old-fashioned oats

1   cup whole wheat flour

2   tablespoons vegetable oil

2   teaspoons salt

1   cup chopped walnuts

1   egg

2   tablespoons milk

     Additional old-fashioned oats

Stir warm water and honey in large bowl to blend. Sprinkle yeast over. Let stand until foamy, about 8 minutes. Heat buttermilk in small saucepan to lukewarm (about 100°F). Stir into yeast mixture. Add 2 cups bread flour, 2 cups oats, wheat flour, oil and salt and stir until smooth. Gradually mix in enough remaining bread flour to form dough. Cover and let dough rest 15 minutes.

Turn out dough onto floured surface. Knead until smooth and elastic, adding more bread flour if sticky, about 10 minutes. Knead in nuts. Oil large bowl. Add dough; turn to coat. Cover bowl with towel; let rise in warm area until doubled, about 50 minutes.

Oil large baking sheet. Punch down dough. Turn out onto oiled surface; knead briefly. Divide dough into 3 pieces. Roll each piece into 16-inch-long rope. Braid ropes together; tuck ends under and pinch to seal. Transfer to prepared sheet. Cover with clean towel. Let rise in warm area until almost doubled, about 45 minutes.

Preheat oven to 375°F. Whisk egg and milk in bowl. Brush loaf generously with some of egg mixture. Sprinkle with additional oats. Bake until golden and tester inserted into center comes out clean, about 50 minutes. Transfer to rack; cool. *(Can be made 1 day ahead. Wrap tightly; store at room temperature.)*

MAKES 1 LOAF

◆ ◆ ◆

These wholesome buttermilk braids are pictured opposite (top) with rounds of Irish Wheat Bread (page 164), and loaves of Colonial Brown Bread (page 164).

◆ ◆ ◆

Irish Wheat Bread

◆ ◆ ◆

2	cups all purpose flour
2	cups whole wheat flour
1	tablespoon baking powder
1	teaspoon baking soda
1	teaspoon salt
1	cup currants or raisins
1¾	cups buttermilk
¼	cup (½ stick) butter, melted
1	large egg, beaten to blend

Preheat oven to 375°F. Grease two 8-inch-diameter cake pans. Stir first 5 ingredients in large bowl. Stir in currants. Whisk buttermilk, butter and egg in small bowl. Add to dry ingredients and stir just until combined. Knead mixture briefly in bowl until dough comes together. Turn out dough onto floured surface and knead until smooth, approximately 2 minutes.

Divide dough into 2 pieces. Shape each into round loaf. Transfer to prepared pans. Using sharp knife, cut an X on surface of each loaf, cutting about ½ inch deep. Bake until tester inserted into center comes out clean, about 50 minutes. Turn out loaves onto racks; cool. *(Can be prepared up to 1 day ahead. Wrap loaves in plastic; store at room temperature.)*

MAKES 2 LOAVES

Colonial Brown Bread

◆ ◆ ◆

◆ ◆ ◆

Like steamed Boston brown bread, this baked version is quickly mixed together and makes a dense, fragrant loaf. The addition of rye flour, which you can find at natural and specialty foods stores, along with some supermarkets, adds an interesting taste.

◆ ◆ ◆

1	cup whole wheat flour
¾	cup raisins
¾	cup coarsely chopped walnuts
⅔	cup all purpose flour
½	cup rye flour*
½	cup yellow cornmeal
½	cup packed golden brown sugar
2	teaspoons baking soda
1	teaspoon ground cinnamon
½	teaspoon ground allspice

½   teaspoon salt
¼   teaspoon ground ginger
⅛   teaspoon ground cloves
2   cups buttermilk
¼   cup dark molasses

Preheat oven to 350°F. Lightly grease two 8½ x 4½ x 2½-inch loaf pans. Stir first 13 ingredients in large bowl to blend. Whisk buttermilk and molasses in small bowl. Mix into dry ingredients.

Divide batter between prepared pans. Bake until tester inserted into center comes out clean, about 40 minutes. Cool in pans on racks 15 minutes. Turn out loaves onto racks and cool. (*Can be made 1 day ahead. Wrap tightly in plastic; store at room temperature.*)

Rye flour is available at natural foods stores, specialty foods stores and also at some supermarkets.

MAKES 2 LOAVES

Sage Focaccia

◆ ◆ ◆

1   1-pound loaf frozen bread dough, thawed
6   tablespoons chopped fresh sage
3   tablespoons olive oil
¾   cup coarsely grated Pecorino Romano cheese (about 2¼ ounces)
    Fresh sage leaves

Place dough in medium bowl. Add 3 tablespoons chopped fresh sage, 1 tablespoon olive oil and generous amount of ground pepper. Knead in bowl to incorporate. Let dough rest 10 minutes. Press out dough on generously floured surface to 12 x 9-inch oval. Transfer dough to ungreased baking sheet. Brush dough with 1 tablespoon olive oil. Let dough rise in warm draft-free area 30 minutes.

Preheat oven to 425°F. Lightly dimple dough all over with fingertips. Brush with remaining 1 tablespoon olive oil. Bake 10 minutes. Sprinkle dough with remaining 3 tablespoons chopped fresh sage, then grated Romano cheese. Bake bread until edges are brown, about 7 minutes longer. Serve bread hot, warm or at room temperature; garnish with fresh sage leaves.

4 TO 6 SERVINGS

EASIEST BREADS EVER

There are any number of uses for frozen bread dough, the focaccia at left being only one of them. And the best thing about the suggestions here? They'll all fill your kitchen with the heavenly small of home-baked bread.

◆ Easy Dinner Rolls: Cut a loaf into 12 pieces, shape each into a ball and arrange in a round cake pan. Brush with melted butter and sprinkle with dill, Parmesan cheese and onion, and poppy seeds or sesame seeds and bake.

◆ Cinnamon Swirl Raisin Bread: Roll dough out into a large rectangle, brush with melted butter and sprinkle with cinnamon, raisins and nuts. Roll up, twist and cut to make two 6-inch pieces, then twist pieces together and bake.

◆ Herb Pretzels: Roll dough out to 5 x 8-inch rectangle, cut with pizza cutter into long ropes and twist each into a pretzel shape. Brush with egg wash and sprinkle with a mix of rosemary, thyme and basil, then coarse salt, and bake.

◆ Three-Cheese Pizza: Roll dough out into a large rectangle. Sprinkle with shredded mozzarella, crumbled Gorgonzola and herbs. Top with sliced tomatoes, grated Parmesan cheese and then bake.

◆ ◆ ◆

Fig Rye Bread

2	cups warm water (105°F to 115°F)
1	package dry yeast
½	teaspoon sugar
1	tablespoon vegetable oil
1	tablespoon salt
3⅔	cups (about) all purpose flour
2	cups whole grain rye flour*
2½	cups diced dried black Mission figs or Calimyrna figs (about 12 ounces)

Place warm water in large bowl. Sprinkle yeast and sugar over water; stir to dissolve. Let stand until foamy, about 8 minutes.

Add oil and salt to yeast mixture. Gradually stir in 3⅓ cups all purpose flour and 2 cups rye flour. Knead dough on floured surface until smooth and elastic, adding up to ⅓ cup more all purpose flour if dough is sticky, approximately 10 minutes.

Grease large bowl. Add dough, turning to coat. Cover with plastic wrap, then kitchen towel. Let dough rise in warm draft-free area until doubled in volume, about 1 hour 15 minutes.

Dust 2 large baking sheets with all purpose flour. Punch down dough. Turn out dough onto lightly floured surface. Press out dough to 1-inch-thick rectangle. Sprinkle figs over. Roll up dough jelly roll style. Knead to distribute figs evenly. Divide dough in half. Roll each piece between work surface and hands into 16-inch-long loaf. Transfer to prepared sheets. Cover with towel. Let rise in warm draft-free area until doubled, about 45 minutes.

Preheat oven to 400°F. Bake loaves until golden and bottoms sound hollow when tapped, using spray bottle to spray oven with water every 10 minutes, approximately 45 minutes. Cool loaves completely on baking sheets on racks.

Whole grain rye flour is available at natural foods stores, specialty foods stores and some supermarkets across the country.

MAKES 2 LARGE LOAVES

Multi-Grain Bread with Sesame, Flax and Poppy Seeds

◆ ◆ ◆

½ cup unsweetened multi-grain cereal (such as 7-grain)
2 cups boiling water

1 envelope dry yeast
4⅓ cups (about) bread flour
1 tablespoon olive oil
1 tablespoon dark brown sugar
1½ teaspoons salt

2 teaspoons sesame seeds
2 teaspoons flax seeds*
2 teaspoons poppy seeds

2 cups water

Place cereal in large bowl. Pour 2 cups boiling water over. Let stand until mixture cools to between 105°F and 115°F, 20 minutes.

Sprinkle yeast over cereal. Add 1 cup bread flour, oil, sugar and salt and stir until smooth. Gradually mix in enough remaining bread flour to form dough. Cover dough; let rest 15 minutes.

Turn out dough onto floured surface. Knead until smooth and elastic, adding more flour if sticky, about 10 minutes. Oil large bowl. Add dough to bowl; turn to coat. Cover bowl with towel. Let dough rise in warm area until doubled, about 1 hour.

Mix all seeds in bowl. Punch down dough. Turn out onto lightly oiled surface. Knead briefly. Shape into 12 x 4-inch loaf. Sprinkle baking sheet with 2 teaspoons seeds. Place loaf atop seeds. Cover with towel. Let loaf rise in warm draft-free area until almost doubled, approximately 30 minutes.

Position 1 oven rack in center and 1 just below center in oven. Place baking pan on lower rack and preheat oven to 425°F. Brush loaf with water. Sprinkle with remaining seed mixture. Using sharp knife, cut 3 diagonal slashes in surface of loaf. Place baking sheet with loaf in oven. Immediately pour 2 cups water into hot pan on lower rack in oven (water will steam).

Bake loaf until golden and tester inserted into center comes out clean, about 35 minutes. Transfer to rack and cool. *(Can be made 1 day ahead. Wrap loaf in plastic; store at room temperature.)*
*Available at natural foods stores.

MAKES 1 LOAF

COOKING WITH SEEDS

Whole seeds, with their concentrated flavor and crunch value, add taste and texture to foods both sweet and savory. Here's a sampling of some of the lesser-known varieties.

◆ Aniseed: A favorite of the ancient Romans, the humble aniseed packs a powerful licorice-like flavor. It's used in cakes and cookies.

◆ Cumin: In medieval Europe, it was believed that cumin could prevent chickens—and husbands—from straying. These days it flavors soups, meats and breads.

◆ Flax: Prized throughout the world for its buttery flavor, the tiny flax seed has been used as a food for centuries. Today we recognize flax seeds as a rich source of heart-friendly omega-3 oils.

◆ Poppy: These bluish-tinted seeds add a nut-like flavor and crunch to everything from hot buttered noodles to salad dressings.

◆ Sesame: One of the world's oldest flavorings, sesame seed was brought to this country by slaves from Africa, who called it "benne seed" and considered it a symbol of good luck. When lightly toasted, it takes on an almond-like flavor.

◆ ◆ ◆

ABOUT WILD RICE

For more than a thousand years, Minnesota's native Chippewas have been gathering at the close of every summer to harvest wild rice—actually the seed of a tall aquatic grass that grows in the silty sediment of the Upper Great Lakes waterways. Because the process of harvesting, drying and winnowing has always been so labor intensive, and because the wild-growing crop has never been a sure thing, wild rice was for many years an expensive commodity, used sparingly to add richness to dishes.

The introduction, in the 1960s, of a variety of wild rice that could be cultivated under controlled conditions resulted in lower prices and a plentiful supply of this delicious grain. Now, wild rice is grown successfully not only in Minnesota but also in other parts of the country as well. Purists, though, still swear by the Chippewas' hand-harvested variety, which they say has a more distinctive flavor. It also happens to cook significantly faster (20 minutes versus 45 minutes for the cultivated kind).

◆ ◆ ◆

Dakota Seed Bread

◆ ◆ ◆

½	cup wild rice
2½	cups warm water (105°F to 115°F)
2	tablespoons honey
1	envelope dry yeast
3	cups whole wheat flour
1	cup nonfat dry milk powder
¾	cup toasted shelled sunflower seeds
½	cup toasted wheat germ
¼	cup vegetable oil
2	teaspoons salt
2½	cups (about) bread flour
1	large egg beaten with 2 tablespoons water

Cook rice in medium pot of boiling salted water until very tender, about 40 minutes. Drain. Cool completely.

Stir warm water and honey in large bowl. Sprinkle yeast over; let stand until foamy, about 8 minutes. Add rice, whole wheat flour, dry milk, ½ cup sunflower seeds, wheat germ, oil and salt and stir until well blended. Gradually mix in enough bread flour to form dough. Cover dough and let rest 15 minutes.

Turn out dough onto floured surface. Knead until smooth and elastic, adding more bread flour if sticky, about 10 minutes. Oil large bowl. Add dough, turning to coat. Cover bowl with towel. Let dough rise in warm area until doubled, about 1 hour.

Line large baking sheet with parchment. Punch down dough. Turn out onto lightly oiled surface. Knead briefly. Divide dough into 2 pieces. Roll each piece between work surface and palms into 12 x 3-inch loaf. Transfer loaves to oiled baking sheet, spacing evenly. Cover with kitchen towel. Let loaves rise in warm draft-free area until almost doubled, about 45 minutes.

Preheat oven to 375°F. Brush loaves generously with egg mixture. Sprinkle with ¼ cup sunflower seeds. Using sharp knife, cut 3 slashes crosswise in surface of each loaf. Bake until golden and tester inserted into center comes out clean, about 35 minutes. Transfer loaves to racks; cool. *(Can be made 1 day ahead. Wrap in plastic and store at room temperature.)*

MAKES 2 LOAVES

Onion-Fennel Flatbreads

◆ ◆ ◆

¼   cup (½ stick) plus 2 teaspoons unsalted butter, room temperature
1½   cups finely chopped onion

1   cup warm water (105°F to 115°F)
1   envelope quick-rising yeast
1   teaspoon sugar
1¼   teaspoons salt
4   teaspoons fennel seeds
3   cups (about) all purpose flour

Melt ¼ cup butter in heavy medium skillet over medium-low heat. Add onion and sauté until very tender, about 15 minutes. Transfer to large bowl of electric mixer fitted with dough hook.

Add 1 cup warm water to onion. Mix in yeast, sugar and salt. Using mortar and pestle, crush 2 teaspoons fennel seeds. Add to onion mixture. Mix in enough flour ½ cup at a time to form medium-soft dough. Knead dough on floured surface until smooth and elastic, about 4 minutes. Allow dough to remain on floured work surface; cover with towel and let stand until beginning to rise, 20 minutes.

Butter heavy large baking sheet. Knead dough briefly. Divide dough into 4 equal pieces. Form each piece into ball; flatten into ¾-inch-thick round, about 5 inches in diameter. Arrange rounds on prepared baking sheet. Rub tops with remaining 2 teaspoons butter. Sprinkle remaining 2 teaspoons whole fennel seeds evenly over rounds and press gently to adhere. Cover with towel. Let rise in warm draft-free area until puffy, about 30 minutes.

Meanwhile, preheat oven to 425°F. Bake breads until golden, about 25 minutes. Serve warm.

MAKES 4

◆ ◆ ◆

Fast-rising yeast makes these moist, fragrant breads quick and easy to prepare. Serve them warm from the oven, accompanied with butter or with olive oil for dipping.

◆ ◆ ◆

· Desserts ·

When it come to desserts, many of us hold to the old adage about "saving the best for last." A sensational ending to a meal does, indeed, make an enduring impression, as the recipes that follow so enticingly prove.

From this selection of the year's best desserts, you're sure to find the perfect finale to any meal, no matter the occasion or what courses have come before. There are fresh-tasting fruit desserts, such as Nectarine Cobbler (page 183) and Pink Grapefruit with Cassis (page 180). For something a little richer, try a pudding or a mousse, maybe Cappuccino Creams (page 198) or Orange Custard with Caramel (page 202). And there are cakes ready to make any meal feel like a party, including Chocolate-Orange Pound Cake with Coffee Glaze (page 186) and Lemon Buttermilk Cake with Strawberries (page 188).

Want something chilling on a hot day? Try Mango Sorbet (page 206) or Butter Pecan Ice Cream Pie (page 208). Or how about just a little nibble? Sugar Cookies (page 219), No-Fail Chocolate Chippers (page 213), Orange and Cinnamon Biscotti (page 214) and a host of other homebaked delights will turn even a cup of coffee or tea into a moment to be relished.

Red, White and Blueberry Sundaes, page 210.

Blueberry Sour Cream Pie

◆ ◆ ◆

CRUST

1¼   cups all purpose flour
½   cup (1 stick) chilled unsalted butter, cut into pieces
2   tablespoons sugar
    Pinch of salt
4   tablespoons (about) ice water

FILLING

1   cup sour cream
¾   cup sugar
2½   tablespoons all purpose flour
1   egg, beaten to blend
¾   teaspoon almond extract
¼   teaspoon salt
2½   cups fresh blueberries

TOPPING

6   tablespoons all purpose flour
¼   cup (½ stick) chilled unsalted butter, cut into pieces
⅓   cup chopped pecans
2   tablespoons sugar

FOR CRUST: Blend flour, butter, sugar and salt in processor until coarse meal forms. With machine running, add water by tablespoonfuls until clumps form. Gather into ball. Flatten to disk. Wrap in plastic; chill until firm, at least 30 minutes.

Preheat oven to 400°F. Roll out dough on floured surface to 13-inch round. Transfer to 9-inch glass pie plate. Trim edge to ½-inch overhang. Fold edge under and crimp. Freeze 10 minutes. Line crust with foil; fill with beans or pie weights. Bake until sides are set, about 12 minutes. Remove foil and beans.

FOR FILLING: Mix first 6 ingredients in medium bowl to blend. Mix in blueberries. Spoon into crust. Bake until just set, 25 minutes.

FOR TOPPING: Using fingertips, mix flour and butter in medium bowl until small clumps form. Mix in pecans and sugar. Spoon topping over pie. Bake until topping browns lightly, about 12 minutes. Cool pie to room temperature.

8 SERVINGS

Strawberry and Chocolate Tart

◆ ◆ ◆

CRUST

1   cup all purpose flour

3   tablespoons sugar

¼   teaspoon salt

⅓   cup walnuts (about 1½ ounces)

½   cup (1 stick) chilled unsalted butter, cut into ½-inch pieces

2   egg yolks

⅓   cup (generous) strawberry jam

FILLING

¾   cup plus 2 tablespoons whipping cream

6   ounces bittersweet (not unsweetened) or semisweet chocolate, chopped

2   1-pint baskets strawberries, hulled, halved

FOR CRUST: Combine flour, sugar and salt in processor and mix. Add walnuts; process until chopped. Add butter and cut in using on/off turns until mixture resembles coarse meal. Add yolks and process just until moist clumps form. Gather dough into ball; flatten to disk. Wrap in plastic and chill 30 minutes.

Preheat oven to 375°F. Butter 9-inch-diameter tart pan with removable bottom. Roll out dough between sheets of waxed paper to 11-inch round. Peel off top sheet of paper. Transfer crust to prepared pan, pressing dough firmly to fit pan and patching if necessary. Discard paper. Trim edges of crust. Freeze crust 15 minutes. Bake until golden brown, about 25 minutes. Spread jam in crust. Return to oven and bake until jam sets, 4 minutes. Cool on rack.

FOR FILLING: Heat cream in heavy small saucepan over medium-low heat until tiny bubbles appear around edges. Remove from heat. Add chocolate and stir until melted. Cool until mixture is beginning to thicken but still pourable, stirring occasionally, 50 minutes.

Pour chocolate filling into crust. Refrigerate until filling is set, about 1 hour 45 minutes. *(Can be prepared 1 day ahead. Cover tart with plastic and keep refrigerated.)*

Arrange strawberries cut side down in concentric circles atop filling. Serve immediately or refrigerate up to 1 hour.

6 TO 8 SERVINGS

◆ ◆ ◆

This rich treat combines a crunchy walnut crust, a creamy chocolate ganache filling and a garnish of ripe strawberries—what could be bad? That, and it can be prepared a day ahead and refrigerated.

Chocolate Raspberry Tart

♦ ♦ ♦

CRUST

1   cup unbleached all purpose flour

¼   cup sugar

3   tablespoons unsweetened cocoa powder

¼   teaspoon salt

6   tablespoons (¾ stick) chilled unsalted butter, cut into pieces

1½   tablespoons cold water

1   large egg yolk

6   tablespoons raspberry jam

FILLING

1   cup whipping cream

4   ounces bittersweet (not unsweetened) or semisweet chocolate, finely chopped

2   ½-pint baskets fresh raspberries

1   teaspoon powdered sugar

1   teaspoon unsweetened cocoa powder

FOR CRUST: Combine flour, sugar, cocoa and salt in medium bowl. Add butter and rub in, using fingertips, until mixture resembles coarse meal. Add water and egg yolk and mix in with fork until well incorporated. Gather dough into rectangle and refrigerate 20 minutes. *(Can be prepared 4 days ahead. Let dough soften slightly at room temperature before rolling out.)*

Preheat oven to 375°F. Butter and flour 13¾ x 4-inch rectangular tart pan with 1-inch-high sides and removable bottom. Roll out dough between 2 sheets of waxed paper to 15 x 6-inch rectangle. Peel off 1 waxed paper sheet. Invert dough into prepared pan; press evenly to fit. Freeze until firm, about 10 minutes. Peel off second waxed paper sheet. Trim edges.

Line crust with foil; fill with dried beans or pie weights. Bake until crust is set, about 12 minutes. Remove foil and beans. Bake until crust just begins to darken around edges, piercing with toothpick if crust bubbles, about 12 minutes longer. Remove from oven; maintain oven temperature. Spread jam over bottom of crust. Bake until jam is set, about 3 minutes. Transfer pan to rack; cool.

FOR FILLING: Bring cream to boil in heavy small saucepan. Remove from heat. Add chocolate and whisk until melted and smooth. Transfer chocolate ganache to bowl and refrigerate until chilled but not firm, about 45 minutes.

Using electric mixer, beat ganache until very thick and semi-firm. Spread ganache over jam in crust. *(Can be prepared 8 hours ahead. Refrigerate.)* Arrange raspberries atop ganache. Stir powdered sugar and cocoa in bowl. Sift over tart.

6 SERVINGS

Pine Nut, Honey and Anise Tart

◆ ◆ ◆

1   15-ounce package refrigerated pie crusts, room temperature
1   teaspoon all purpose flour

½   cup honey
½   cup sugar
1   egg, beaten to blend
3   tablespoons anisette (anise-flavored liqueur)
1   teaspoon aniseed, ground in mortar with pestle
¼   teaspoon salt
5   tablespoons unsalted butter, melted
1   cup pine nuts

Preheat oven to 450°F. Unfold 1 crust and peel off plastic. Press out fold lines. If crust cracks, wet fingers and push edges together. Sprinkle crust with flour and, using fingers, spread flour over entire crust. Place crust floured side down in 9-inch-diameter tart pan with removable bottom. Fold overhang in and build up edges about ¼ inch above rim of pan. Pierce all over with fork. Bake until light brown, 12 minutes. Patch any cracks using second crust, if necessary. Cool on rack. Reduce oven temperature to 350°F.

Mix honey, sugar, egg, anisette, aniseed and salt in medium bowl. Stir in butter and nuts. Pour mixture into crust. Bake until top is dark brown (filling will set as it cools), about 40 minutes. Cool on rack. *(Can be made 8 hours ahead. Let stand at room temperature.)*

8 SERVINGS

◆ ◆ ◆

When starting out on this easy-to-make tart, be sure to thaw both packaged pie crusts. Use one for the crust itself and the other to patch and repair any cracks that may appear in the tart crust during baking.

◆ ◆ ◆

Lemon Cream and Raspberry Phyllo Napoleons

◆ ◆ ◆

PHYLLO SQUARES

6   fresh phyllo pastry sheets or frozen, thawed

6   teaspoons (generous) sugar

2   tablespoons unsalted butter, melted

LEMON CREAM

½   cup chilled whipping cream

1½ teaspoons powdered sugar

½   teaspoon vanilla extract

¼   cup purchased lemon curd

2   ½-pint baskets fresh raspberries or 2 cups frozen unsweetened, thawed, drained
Powdered sugar

◆ ◆ ◆

In this quick and easy take on the napoleon, crisp phyllo pastry squares are layered with lemon cream and raspberries. Jars of ready-made lemon curd are available in the preserves section of most supermarkets.

◆ ◆ ◆

FOR PHYLLO SQUARES: Preheat oven to 375°F. Lightly oil 2 large baking sheets. Stack phyllo sheets on work surface. Trim to 10½-inch square (reserve scraps for another use). Place 1 phyllo square on work surface (cover remaining phyllo with plastic wrap and damp kitchen towel). Sprinkle with 1 generous teaspoon sugar. Top with second phyllo square. Brush lightly with melted unsalted butter. Sprinkle with 1 generous teaspoon sugar. Top with third phyllo square. Sprinkle with 1 generous teaspoon sugar. Cut phyllo

stack into 9 equal stacked squares. Arrange stacked phyllo squares on prepared baking sheet. Repeat layering and cutting with remaining 3 phyllo sheets, sugar and butter making total of 18 stacked phyllo squares. Bake until phyllo is golden, about 10 minutes. Transfer baking sheets to racks and cool completely.

FOR LEMON CREAM: Beat cream, 1½ teaspoons powdered sugar and vanilla in large bowl until medium peaks form. Whisk lemon curd in another medium bowl until smooth. Add to cream mixture. Beat lemon cream to stiff peaks.

Spread 1 generous tablespoon lemon cream on each of 6 stacked phyllo squares. Top each with 6 raspberries. Layer each with 1 phyllo square, 1 more tablespoon lemon cream and 6 raspberries (save any remaining lemon cream for another use). Top each with 1 phyllo square. Sift powdered sugar over desserts. *(Can be prepared 8 hours ahead. Cover loosely and refrigerate.)*

MAKES 6

Raspberry Jam Tart

◆ ◆ ◆

1   sheet frozen puff pastry (half of 17¼-ounce package), thawed
¼   cup seedless raspberry jam
1   large egg
1   tablespoon whipping cream

Preheat oven to 375°F. Roll out pastry on floured surface to 12 x 9-inch rectangle. Cut pastry in half lengthwise, creating two 12 x 4½-inch strips. Place 1 pastry strip on large baking sheet. Spread jam evenly over pastry, leaving ½-inch border on all sides. Fold remaining pastry strip in half lengthwise. Using small knife and beginning ½ inch from 1 end of pastry, cut slit through fold to within ½ inch of unfolded side of pastry. Repeat cutting slits at ½-inch intervals. Unfold dough and open flat on work surface. Whisk egg and cream in small mixing bowl to blend. Brush cut pastry with some of egg mixture. Brush edges of jam-covered pastry strip with some of egg mixture. Place cut pastry strip over strip with jam, egg-glazed side up. Press edges of tart firmly to seal.

Bake tart until pastry is golden, about 25 minutes. Transfer sheet to rack and cool 5 minutes. Using large metal spatula, loosen tart from sheet. Slide tart onto rack and cool completely. *(Can be prepared 6 hours ahead. Cover and let stand at room temperature.)*

6 SERVINGS

◆ ◆ ◆

Use store-bought puff pastry and raspberry jam for this speedy version of the classic French *jalousie* tart. And make it up to six hours ahead.

◆ ◆ ◆

Bake-Sale Lemon Meringue Pie

◆ ◆ ◆

1   refrigerated pie crust (half of 15-ounce package), room temperature
1   teaspoon all purpose flour

1¼   cups plus ⅓ cup sugar
1½   cups water
6   tablespoons cornstarch
5   large eggs, separated
1   tablespoon grated lemon peel
     Pinch of salt
½   cup fresh lemon juice
2   tablespoons (¼ stick) unsalted butter, room temperature

½   teaspoon cream of tartar

Position rack in center of oven and preheat to 450°F. Unfold pie crust. Press out fold lines. If crust cracks, wet fingers and push edges together. Sprinkle flour over crust. Place crust floured side down in 9-inch-diameter glass pie dish. Fold edges over; crimp decoratively. Pierce crust all over with fork. Bake until crust is pale golden, about 12 minutes. Cool crust completely on rack.

Whisk 1¼ cups sugar, water, 5 tablespoons cornstarch, egg yolks, lemon peel and salt in heavy medium saucepan to blend. Whisk over medium heat until mixture comes to boil. Whisk until mixture thickens, about 2 minutes. Remove from heat. Add lemon juice and butter; whisk until smooth. Cool lemon filling completely, stirring occasionally, about 1 hour.

Preheat oven to 350°F. Mix ⅓ cup sugar and 1 tablespoon cornstarch in small bowl. Beat egg whites in large bowl until foamy; add cream of tartar and beat until soft peaks form. Add sugar and cornstarch mixture 1 tablespoonful at a time, beating until stiff peaks form after each addition. Set meringue aside.

Spread cooled lemon filling in crust. Spoon dollops of meringue around edge of pie atop filling. Spoon remaining meringue onto center of pie. Spread meringue to cover filling, mounding in center and sealing completely to crust edge. Using rubber spatula or spoon, swirl meringue decoratively, forming peaks. Bake pie until meringue peaks are light brown, about 12 minutes. Transfer to rack and cool completely. Refrigerate pie until cold, about 1½ hours. *(Can be prepared 3 hours ahead. Keep refrigerated.)*

8 SERVINGS

In the good old days, when everyone baked, the bake sale offered cooks a chance to strut their stuff. The competition was friendly but cutthroat, and winners were determined by whose sweets sold first—and at what premium price. In celebration of those leisurely days, here is a prizewinning lemon meringue pie.

◆ ◆ ◆

Apricot and Cherry Country Tart

◆ ◆ ◆

CRUST

1   cup all purpose flour

⅛   teaspoon sugar

    Pinch of salt

6   tablespoons (¾ stick) chilled unsalted butter, cut into pieces

2½ tablespoons (about) ice water

FILLING

2   tablespoons all purpose flour

2   teaspoons plus 4½ tablespoons sugar

8   large apricots, halved, pitted

1   cup pitted cherries (about 6 ounces) or frozen, thawed

2   tablespoons (¼ stick) unsalted butter, melted, cooled

    Vanilla ice cream or frozen yogurt

FOR CRUST: Stir flour, ⅛ teaspoon sugar and salt in bowl. Add butter; rub in with fingertips until coarse meal forms. Mix in enough water by tablespoonfuls until clumps form. Gather into ball; flatten into disk. Wrap in plastic; chill at least 1 hour and up to 2 days.

Preheat oven to 400°F. Line baking sheet with parchment. Roll out dough on floured surface to 11-inch round. Transfer to sheet.

FOR FILLING: Mix flour and 2 teaspoons sugar in bowl. Sprinkle over crust, leaving 1½-inch border. Place apricots cut side down on crust, placing close together and leaving 1½-inch border at outer edge. Scatter cherries over apricots. Top with 4 tablespoons sugar. Fold pastry edges up around apricots, pressing against apricots to form scalloped border. Brush crust with butter; sprinkle with remaining ½ tablespoon sugar.

Bake until crust is golden and fruit is tender (some juices from fruit will leak onto parchment), about 1 hour. Remove from oven. Using pastry brush, brush tart with juices on parchment. Gently slide parchment with tart onto rack. Carefully run long knife under tart to loosen (crust is fragile). Cool on parchment until lukewarm. Slide 9-inch-diameter tart pan bottom under tart, then place tart on platter. Serve with ice cream or yogurt.

6 SERVINGS

ABOUT CASSIS

Cassis is the French term for black currants, and it was the French who introduced crème de cassis, a potently sweet aperitif, which is made from the juice of black currants blended with brandy and sugar. Cassis is often used as a base for cocktails of different kinds, including the Vermouth Cassis, a blend of cassis, vermouth and soda water served over ice.

But cassis is more than a drink ingredient, adding its deep rich essence to light custards, soufflés and fruit tarts. Just a drizzle works wonders with a bowl of fresh berries. Here, it gets stirred into a sweet syrup and spooned over grapefruit segments (pictured opposite with the Sesame-Almond Macaroons from page 215), and mixed with lemon curd for a sauce to top oranges and strawberries. Experiment by adding cassis to your favorite fruit recipes. Just remember that it's a fairly intense flavoring, and a little goes a long way.

◆ ◆ ◆

Pink Grapefruit with Cassis

◆ ◆ ◆

2	large pink grapefruits (about 14 ounces each)
2	tablespoons sugar
1½	tablespoons water
2	tablespoons crème de cassis
	Fresh mint sprigs (optional)

Using small sharp knife, remove peel and white pith from grapefruits. Working over bowl to catch juice, cut between membranes to release segments. Reserve juice in bowl. Arrange grapefruit segments decoratively on 4 plates, dividing equally.

Combine sugar, water and reserved grapefruit juice in heavy small saucepan. Stir over low heat until sugar dissolves. Remove saucepan from heat. Stir in crème de cassis. Drizzle syrup over grapefruit. Refrigerate at least 2 hours or up to 6 hours. Garnish with mint sprigs, if desired, and serve chilled.

4 SERVINGS

Fruit with Cassis-spiked Lemon Curd Sauce

◆ ◆ ◆

½	cup purchased lemon curd
2	tablespoons crème de cassis
½	cup plain yogurt, crème fraîche or sour cream (not low-fat or nonfat)
3	oranges, peel and white pith removed, fruit sliced, slices quartered
1	1-pint basket strawberries, hulled, halved
	Fresh mint sprigs

Whisk lemon curd and crème de cassis in small bowl to blend. Stir in yogurt. *(Sauce can be prepared 2 days ahead. Chill.)*

Combine oranges and strawberries in medium bowl. Spoon fruit into balloon glasses. Spoon sauce over. Garnish with mint sprigs.

4 SERVINGS

Baked Pears with Honey and Ginger

♦ ♦ ♦

Nonstick vegetable oil spray
8   firm but ripe Bartlett pears, peeled, halved, cored
1   cup packed golden brown sugar
3   teaspoons ground ginger
6   tablespoons honey
3   tablespoons fresh lemon juice
2   teaspoons grated lemon peel
10 tablespoons (1¼ sticks) unsalted butter

1   quart vanilla frozen yogurt
Fresh mint sprigs (optional)
Lemon peel strips (optional)

Preheat oven to 375°F. Spray 2 large ovenproof skillets with oil spray. Arrange half of pears cut side down in each skillet. Sprinkle ½ cup sugar and 1½ teaspoons ginger over pears in each skillet. Mix honey, lemon juice and peel in small bowl. Drizzle over pears. Dot pears in each skillet with 3 tablespoons butter.

Place skillets with pears in oven. Bake until juices bubble thickly and pears are tender when pierced with small sharp knife, basting occasionally, about 15 minutes. Turn pears over. Bake 5 minutes longer. Remove pears from oven. (*Can be made 1 day ahead.*

Cool. Transfer pears and cooking syrup to large glass baking dish; cover and chill. Rewarm pears uncovered in 375°F oven 15 minutes before continuing with recipe.)

Arrange 2 pear halves on each of 8 plates. Transfer cooking syrup to 1 large skillet. Bring syrup to simmer; whisk in 4 tablespoons butter. Spoon over pears. Place 1 scoop yogurt alongside. Garnish with mint and lemon peel, if desired.

8 SERVINGS

Nectarine Cobbler

◆ ◆ ◆

FILLING

4	pounds nectarines, cut into wedges
¾	cup plus 2 tablespoons sugar
⅓	cup unbleached all purpose flour
2	tablespoons fresh lemon juice

TOPPING

2¼	cups unbleached all purpose flour
6	tablespoons sugar
1	tablespoon baking powder
¾	teaspoon salt
¼	cup (½ stick) chilled unsalted butter, cut into pieces
¼	cup chilled solid vegetable shortening, cut into pieces
1	large egg, beaten to blend
¾	cup plus 2 tablespoons chilled buttermilk
	Vanilla ice cream

FOR FILLING: Position rack in center of oven and preheat to 400°F. Mix nectarines, sugar, flour and lemon juice in 13 x 9 x 2-inch glass baking dish. Bake 15 minutes.

MEANWHILE, PREPARE TOPPING: Mix flour, 4 tablespoons sugar, baking powder and salt in large bowl. Using fingertips, rub in butter and shortening until mixture resembles coarse meal. Add egg and buttermilk; stir until batter forms.

Remove fruit from oven. Spoon batter over hot filling in 12 mounds, spacing evenly. Sprinkle with 2 tablespoons sugar. Bake until juices thicken and topping is golden, about 30 minutes. Cool on rack at least 15 minutes. Serve warm with vanilla ice cream.

8 SERVINGS

◆ ◆ ◆

This may be the quintessential summer treat. It comes together quickly (nectarines rarely need peeling), and tastes fresh as the fruit itself. When it's warm, ice cream seems the perfect go-with, but some softly whipped and sweetened cream would also be delicious.

◆ ◆ ◆

CRISPS, COBBLERS AND MORE

Crisps, cobblers, grunts, slumps, buckles and Bettys—these are some of the names used to describe early New England's homespun fruit desserts. These simple sweets took advantage of seasonal plenty, transforming fresh apples, peaches, berries and cherries into cooked treats that were served with fresh cream for dessert.

Grunts and slumps are fruit topped with dollops of biscuit dough and steamed on top of the stove. Cobblers are likewise topped with a rich biscuit crust, which was pressed into the fruit mixture in pieces for a "cobbled" effect and then baked in the oven. Buckles get a solid biscuit "lid" that bubbles and bulges during baking.

Fashioned much like a pie, a pandowdy is made up of a fruit filling encased in two flaky crusts. During the last hour of baking, the top crust is "dowdied" by being cut into the fruit with a sharp knife.

Crisps, crunches and Brown Bettys tend to be all of a kind and feature buttery crumb crusts. Sometimes the topping is layered with the fruit for a heartier texture. Occasionally, oatmeal is mixed in for a crunchier crust.

◆ ◆ ◆

Apple-Cranberry Crisp

◆ ◆ ◆

1½   pounds tart green apples, peeled, cored, cut into ¾-inch pieces
3   cups fresh or frozen cranberries
⅔   cup sugar
4   tablespoons all purpose flour
1   teaspoon ground cinnamon
½   teaspoon ground nutmeg

¾   cup old-fashioned rolled oats
2   tablespoons firmly packed golden brown sugar
3   tablespoons butter, cut into pieces, room temperature
    Vanilla frozen yogurt

Preheat oven to 375°F. Toss apples, cranberries, ⅔ cup sugar, 2 tablespoons flour, cinnamon and nutmeg to blend in large bowl. Transfer to 8 x 8 x 2-inch glass baking dish. Let stand 15 minutes.

Combine oats, brown sugar and remaining 2 tablespoons flour in medium bowl. Add butter and stir until moist clumps form. Sprinkle topping over filling. Bake until topping is golden brown and filling bubbles, about 1 hour. Cool slightly. Serve warm or at room temperature with frozen yogurt.

6 SERVINGS

Melon and Blueberry Coupe with White Wine, Vanilla and Mint

◆ ◆ ◆

1½   cups dry white wine
½   cup sugar
1   vanilla bean, split lengthwise

2⅓   cups cantaloupe cubes (about ½ melon)
2⅓   cups honeydew cubes (about ½ small melon)
2⅓   cups watermelon cubes (about ¼ small melon)
3   cups fresh blueberries (about 1½ half-pint baskets)
½   cup chopped fresh mint

Combine ½ cup wine and sugar in small saucepan. Scrape in seeds from vanilla bean; add bean. Stir over low heat until sugar dissolves and syrup is hot, about 2 minutes. Remove from heat and let steep 30 minutes. Remove vanilla bean from syrup.

Combine all fruit in large bowl. Add mint and remaining 1 cup wine to sugar syrup. Pour over fruit. Cover and refrigerate at least 2 hours. *(Can be prepared 6 hours ahead. Keep refrigerated.)*

Spoon fruit and some syrup into large stemmed goblets.

6 SERVINGS

Perfumed Oranges

◆ ◆ ◆

6	navel oranges
⅓	cup honey
¼	cup orange juice
1	tablespoon orange flower water*
1	teaspoon ground cinnamon
	Mint sprigs (optional)

Using small sharp knife, cut peel and white pith from all oranges. Slice oranges into thin rounds. Arrange orange slices in shallow glass baking dish. Stir honey, orange juice and orange blossom water in heavy small saucepan over medium heat until honey melts. Pour honey mixture over orange slices. Refrigerate at least 1 hour and up to 4 hours, basting orange slices occasionally.

Arrange orange slices decoratively on large serving platter. Spoon honey sauce over. Sprinkle with ground cinnamon. Garnish orange slices with mint sprigs, if desired.

A flavoring extract available at liquor stores and in the liquor or specialty foods sections of some supermarkets.

6 SERVINGS

◆ ◆ ◆

Orange flower water, a unique flavoring extract, provides the "perfume" in this simple dessert. Serve the fruit with the Orange Blossom Almond Crescents from page 217.

Chocolate-Orange Pound Cake with Coffee Glaze

◆ ◆ ◆

◆ ◆ ◆

A good chocolate pound cake is as versatile as a basic black dress. You can accessorize it with the glaze or simply dust it with powdered sugar. You can serve it for dessert at a dinner party or pack it for a picnic. You can give it as a gift or freeze it (for up to two months) for those times when unexpected guests drop by. All that, and this treat is low in fat, too.

◆ ◆ ◆

Nonstick vegetable oil spray
1   cup plus 2 tablespoons sifted all purpose flour
6   tablespoons unsweetened Dutch-process cocoa powder
½   teaspoon baking soda
¼   teaspoon baking powder
¼   teaspoon salt
1   large egg
2   large egg whites
2   tablespoons warm water
1   tablespoon instant espresso powder or instant coffee powder
1   teaspoon vanilla extract
6   tablespoons nonfat plain yogurt

6   tablespoons (¾ stick) unsalted butter, room temperature
1   teaspoon grated orange peel
1⅓ cups sugar

½   cup powdered sugar
2   tablespoons coffee liqueur

Preheat oven to 350°F. Spray 6- to 8-cup tube or Bundt pan with vegetable oil spray. Sift flour, cocoa, baking soda, baking powder and salt into medium bowl. Whisk egg and egg whites to blend in small bowl. Stir water, espresso powder and vanilla in another small bowl until powder dissolves; mix in yogurt.

Using electric mixer, beat butter and peel in large bowl for 1 minute. Gradually add sugar, beating until blended, about 3 minutes. Gradually pour eggs into butter mixture, beating until smooth, about 3 minutes. At low speed, add flour mixture alternately with yogurt mixture in 3 additions each, beating just until combined after each addition and scraping down sides. Transfer to prepared pan.

Bake cake until tester inserted near center comes out clean, about 40 minutes. Cool cake in pan on rack 10 minutes. Turn out cake onto rack; cool completely.

Stir powdered sugar and liqueur in small bowl until smooth. Let stand until glaze begins to set up, 30 minutes. Spoon over cake.

12 SERVINGS

Lemon Buttermilk Cake with Strawberries

◆ ◆ ◆

CAKE

1¾ cups sugar

¾ cup (1½ sticks) unsalted butter, room temperature

2 tablespoons grated lemon peel

3 extra-large eggs

¼ cup fresh lemon juice

3 cups cake flour

1 teaspoon baking soda

¼ teaspoon salt

1½ cups buttermilk

1 16-ounce package frozen sliced sweetened strawberries, thawed

FROSTING

12 ounces cream cheese, room temperature

½ cup (1 stick) unsalted butter, room temperature

2 cups powdered sugar

5 tablespoons frozen lemonade concentrate, thawed

½ teaspoon finely grated lemon peel

2 1-pint baskets strawberries, hulled

FOR CAKE: Position rack in center of oven and preheat to 350°F. Butter and flour three 9-inch-diameter cake pans with 1½-inch-high sides. Beat sugar, butter and lemon peel in large bowl until light and fluffy. Add eggs 1 at a time, beating well after each addition. Beat in lemon juice. Sift flour, baking soda and salt into medium bowl. Stir dry ingredients into butter mixture alternately with buttermilk, beginning and ending with dry ingredients.

Divide batter among prepared pans. Bake until tester inserted into center of cakes comes out clean, about 30 minutes. Transfer pans to racks and cool 15 minutes. Turn out cakes onto racks and cool completely. *(Can be prepared 1 day ahead. Wrap tightly in plastic and store at room temperature.)*

Boil sliced sweetened strawberries with juices in heavy small saucepan over medium-high heat until mixture is reduced to ⅔ cup and begins to thicken, stirring frequently, about 20 minutes. Cool strawberry mixture to room temperature.

FOR FROSTING: Beat cream cheese and butter in large bowl until light and fluffy. Gradually add powdered sugar and beat until smooth. Beat in lemonade concentrate and lemon peel.

Divide strawberry mixture between 2 cake layers and spread over tops, leaving ½-inch border around edges. Let stand until slightly set, about 5 minutes. Place 1 strawberry-topped layer on platter. Drop ¾ cup frosting atop cake by spoonfuls; gently spread over top. Top with remaining strawberry-topped layer. Drop ¾ cup frosting by spoonfuls atop cake; gently spread over top. Top with remaining cake layer. Using spatula, spread remaining frosting in decorative swirls over sides and top of cake. *(Can be prepared 1 day ahead. Cover with cake dome and chill. Let cake stand at room temperature 1 hour before continuing.)*

Decoratively arrange strawberries, pointed side up, atop cake. Cut into wedges and serve immediately.

12 SERVINGS

◆ ◆ ◆

Serve this dense, moist cake with a big bowl of lightly sweetened strawberries. Perfect for a festive occasion (a birthday party or a large gathering like the Garden Party on page 83), it can be made a day ahead. Simply garnish before serving.

◆ ◆ ◆

Mocha-Orange Cheesecake

◆ ◆ ◆

CRUST

21   Pepperidge Farm Orange Milano cookies, broken into pieces

¼   cup (½ stick) unsalted butter, cut into ½-inch pieces

1½   teaspoons instant espresso powder

FILLING

4   ounces bittersweet or semisweet chocolate, chopped

2   8-ounce packages cream cheese, room temperature

¾   cup sugar

⅓   cup frozen orange juice concentrate, thawed

2   tablespoons coffee liqueur

2   tablespoons Grand Marnier or other orange liqueur

2   tablespoons instant espresso powder

3   large eggs

TOPPING

1½   cups sour cream

6   tablespoons (packed) powdered sugar

4   teaspoons instant espresso powder

◆ ◆ ◆

Espresso, chocolate and orange star in this very rich, very elegant cheesecake. If you like, garnish it with orange slices and chocolate curls. (Note that the cake needs to be refrigerated at least eight hours and up to two days before serving.)

◆ ◆ ◆

FOR CRUST: Preheat oven to 325°F. Wrap outside of 9-inch-diameter springform pan with 2¾-inch-high sides with foil. Combine all ingredients in processor. Process until moist crumbs form. Press onto bottom and 1½ inches up side of prepared pan. Bake until puffed and brown, 15 minutes; cool. Maintain oven temperature.

FOR FILLING: Melt chocolate in top of double boiler set over simmering water, stirring until smooth. Using electric mixer, beat cream cheese and sugar in large bowl until smooth. Mix in chocolate. Add juice concentrate, liqueurs and espresso; beat until mixture is smooth. Beat in eggs, adding 1 at a time.

Spoon ⅓ cup batter into pastry bag fitted with ¼-inch plain tip; chill. Pour remaining batter into crust. Bake until softly set in center and slightly puffed at edges, about 45 minutes. Let cool 10 minutes. Maintain oven temperature.

FOR TOPPING: Mix sour cream, powdered sugar and espresso powder in small bowl until espresso powder dissolves. Spread over hot cake. Pipe reserved ⅓ cup cake batter in parallel stripes (about ½ inch apart) over topping. Bake cake until topping is set, about 5 minutes. Cut around pan sides to loosen crust. Place cake immediately into refrigerator. Chill completely, about 8 hours and up to 2 days. Cut around pan sides; release.

10 TO 12 SERVINGS

Warm Bittersweet Chocolate Cupcakes with Vanilla Ice Cream

◆ ◆ ◆

½   cup plus 6 tablespoons whipping cream
2   tablespoons (¼ stick) unsalted butter
1   tablespoon unsweetened cocoa powder
8   ounces bittersweet (not unsweetened) chocolate, finely chopped

2   large eggs
¼   cup sugar
¼   cup ground pecans
1   teaspoon vanilla extract

Vanilla ice cream

Preheat oven to 350°F. Butter nine ⅓-cup muffin cups. Sprinkle with sugar; shake out excess. Bring ½ cup cream, butter and cocoa powder to boil in heavy small saucepan, whisking until smooth. Remove from heat. Add 5 ounces chocolate; stir until melted. Cool chocolate mixture for 10 minutes.

Beat eggs and ¼ cup sugar in medium bowl until slowly dissolving ribbon forms when beaters are lifted, about 8 minutes. Gently fold in pecans and vanilla. Fold in chocolate mixture in 2 additions. Divide batter among muffin cups.

Bake cupcakes until puffed and knife inserted into center comes out clean, about 18 minutes. Cool in pan on rack 10 minutes (cake centers will sink). Using small sharp knife, cut around sides of cakes. Turn out cakes. *(Can be made 1 day ahead. Cool cakes completely. Cover and store at room temperature. Reheat uncovered in 350°F oven about 10 minutes.)*

Bring 6 tablespoons cream to boil in small saucepan. Remove from heat. Add 3 ounces chocolate; stir until melted.

Arrange warm cakes upside down on plates. Spoon chocolate glaze over. Serve with vanilla ice cream.

8 SERVINGS

These individual chocolate cakes are best served warm with vanilla ice cream. If you like, drizzle the dessert with caramel sauce just before serving. (The recipe makes nine cupcakes; save the extra one for a snack.)

◆ ◆ ◆

Margarita Cheesecake

◆ ◆ ◆

CRUST

Nonstick vegetable oil spray

1¼ cups graham cracker crumbs

¼ cup (½ stick) unsalted butter, melted

FILLING

3 8-ounce "bricks" Neufchâtel cheese (reduced-fat cream cheese), room temperature

1¼ cups light sour cream

¾ cup plus 2 tablespoons sugar

2½ tablespoons triple sec or other orange liqueur

2½ tablespoons tequila

2½ tablespoons fresh lime juice

4 large eggs

TOPPING

¾ cup light sour cream

1 tablespoon fresh lime juice

1 tablespoon sugar

Very thin lime slices, cut in half
Very thin lime peel strips

FOR CRUST: Position rack in center of oven and preheat to 350°F. Spray 9-inch springform pan with 2¾-inch-high sides with vegetable oil spray. Mix graham cracker crumbs and butter in medium bowl until blended. Press crumbs over bottom and 1 inch up sides of prepared pan. Refrigerate crust.

FOR FILLING: Using electric mixer, beat cheese in large bowl until fluffy. Beat in sour cream, then sugar, triple sec, tequila and lime juice. Beat in eggs. Pour filling into crust. Bake until outside 2 inches are set and center moves only slightly when pan is shaken, about 50 minutes. Remove from oven; turn off oven.

FOR TOPPING: Whisk sour cream, lime juice and sugar in small bowl to blend. Spread evenly over cheesecake. Return to hot oven. Let stand 45 minutes. *(Cheesecake will look very soft but will set up when chilled.)* Refrigerate cake until well chilled, up to 1 day.

Run knife around pan sides. Remove pan sides. Place cake on platter. Arrange lime half-slices and peel around top edge of cake.

10 TO 12 SERVINGS

THE LIGHTER SIDE OF DAIRY

As we get wiser about fat and its effect on our long-term health, we are becoming more familiar with lower-fat alternatives to typically fat-rich dairy products. We're even learning how to use these "lighter" milks, butters, sour creams and cheeses in recipes, as in the deliciously creamy cheesecake at left.

Whole milk weighs in at 3½% milk fat; low-fat milk comes in 1% and 2% versions. If you're really serious about fat, skim or nonfat milk is essentially fat-free. The newest, sometimes called "extra light" milk, has the same amount of fat as 1% milk, but with milk solids added for a creamier taste.

There are low-fat as well as nonfat versions of buttermilk, sour cream and yogurt. Even butter is now available in a "light" version, with water, skim milk or nondairy ingredients added to reduce fat content. Or, try whipped butter, which is less dense than the cube style so it has less fat and fewer calories.

◆ ◆ ◆

Plum Upside-down Cake

♦ ♦ ♦

12 tablespoons (1½ sticks) unsalted butter, room temperature
1   cup packed golden brown sugar
1   tablespoon honey
6   large plums, halved, pitted, each half cut into 6 wedges

1½ cups all purpose flour
2   teaspoons baking powder
½   teaspoon ground cinnamon
¼   teaspoon salt
1   cup sugar
2   large eggs
½   teaspoon vanilla extract
¼   teaspoon almond extract
½   cup milk

Lightly sweetened whipped cream

Preheat oven to 350°F. Stir 6 tablespoons butter, brown sugar and honey in heavy medium skillet over low heat until butter melts and sugar and honey blend in, forming thick, smooth sauce. Transfer to 9-inch-diameter cake pan with 2-inch-high sides. Arrange plums in overlapping concentric circles atop sauce.

Mix flour, baking powder, cinnamon and salt in medium bowl. Using electric mixer, beat remaining 6 tablespoons butter in large bowl until light. Add sugar and beat until creamy. Add eggs and beat until light and fluffy. Beat in extracts. Add dry ingredients alternately with milk, mixing just until blended. Spoon batter evenly over plums. Bake cake until golden and tester inserted into center of cake comes out clean, about 1 hour 5 minutes. Transfer to rack; cool cake in pan on rack for 30 minutes.

Using knife, cut around pan sides to loosen cake. Place platter atop cake pan. Invert cake; place platter on work surface. Let stand 5 minutes. Gently lift off pan. Serve with whipped cream.

8 SERVINGS

♦ ♦ ♦

The good things, like simple, old-fashioned, homey desserts, never go out of fashion. This updated version of an American classic — with plums replacing the expected pineapple — proves the point deliciously.

♦ ♦ ♦

Orange Almond Torte with Orange Sauce and Marsala Cream

◆ ◆ ◆

CAKE

½   cup (1 stick) unsalted butter, room temperature

¾   cup sugar

1   large egg

2   large egg yolks

1   cup almonds, toasted, finely ground

½   cup all purpose flour

2   tablespoons orange juice

1   tablespoon grated orange peel

½   teaspoon ground coriander

   Pinch of salt

2   large egg whites

CREAM

1   cup chilled whipping cream

2   tablespoons powdered sugar

2   tablespoons sweet Marsala

   Additional powdered sugar
   Orange Sauce (see recipe on page 197)

FOR CAKE: Preheat oven to 375°F. Butter 8-inch-diameter springform pan. Line bottom of pan with parchment. Butter parchment; dust with flour. Beat ½ cup butter in large bowl until fluffy. Gradually add sugar, beating until blended. Add egg, then yolks, 1 at a time, beating well after each addition. At low speed, beat in almonds, flour, orange juice, peel, coriander and salt, scraping down sides of bowl occasionally.

Using clean dry beaters, beat whites until stiff but not dry. Fold whites into batter in 2 additions. Transfer to prepared pan.

Bake cake until top is golden and tester comes out clean, about 40 minutes. Cool cake in pan on rack. *(Can be made 1 day ahead. Cover and let stand at room temperature.)*

FOR CREAM: Beat whipping cream and 2 tablespoons sugar in medium bowl until soft peaks form. Mix in Marsala.

Dust cake with powdered sugar. Cut cake into wedges and serve with Marsala cream and Orange Sauce.

6 SERVINGS

◆ ◆ ◆

Ideal for entertaining, this delicate cake can be prepared a day before serving. It works especially well at the end of an Italian-themed menu, such as the one page 124.

◆ ◆ ◆

Orange Sauce

1	cup fresh orange juice
1½	tablespoons cornstarch
2	tablespoons (¼ stick) unsalted butter
¼	cup sugar
1	tablespoon grated orange peel

Whisk juice and cornstarch in bowl until cornstarch dissolves. Melt butter in heavy small saucepan over medium-high heat. Whisk in sugar, orange peel and orange juice mixture. Whisk until sauce boils and thickens slightly, about 4 minutes. Remove from heat and cool. *(Can be made 2 days ahead. Cover and refrigerate. Bring to room temperature before serving.)*

MAKES ABOUT 1¼ CUPS

MORE ON MARSALA

Marsala is a sweet, amber-colored dessert wine that comes from Sicily. It is often used in cooking, lending its delicate essence to sauces for light meats such as veal and chicken, and also as a flavoring in dessert custards and sweet, creamy sauces.

Made from the "must" (grape juice syrup) of aromatic white wines mixed with dried grapes fermented with brandy, Marsala is a blended wine that is aged at least two years in wooden casks before bottling.

While Marsala comes in both inexpensive and costly versions—and everything in between—it can be worth investing in a bottle of the finest aged Marsala, especially if you plan on enjoying a glass of Marsala while you're cooking with it.

◆ ◆ ◆

Cappuccino Creams

◆ ◆ ◆

Nonstick vegetable oil spray

1	2½-inch piece vanilla bean, split lengthwise
1¾	cups whipping cream
2	ounces good-quality white chocolate (such as Lindt or Bakers), finely chopped

5	tablespoons sugar
4	large egg yolks
1	large egg
¼	cup sour cream
4	teaspoons clear (white) rum
	Pinch of salt

4	teaspoons instant espresso powder

Preheat oven to 350°F. Spray six ¾-cup ramekins or custard cups with nonstick spray. Place cups in 13 x 9 x 2-inch baking pan. Scrape seeds from vanilla bean into small saucepan; add bean. Mix in ½ cup cream and white chocolate. Stir over low heat until smooth. Set white choclate mixture aside.

Whisk 1¼ cups cream, sugar, yolks, egg, sour cream, rum and salt in medium bowl until smooth. Strain white chocolate mixture

◆ ◆ ◆

White chocolate custard tops espresso custard in this luxurious make-ahead dessert. It's pretty garnished with fresh strawberries (or any berry) and coffee beans.

◆ ◆ ◆

into egg mixture and whisk to blend. Pour ¼ cup custard mixture into each ramekin; reserve remaining custard. Pour enough hot water into baking pan to come halfway up sides of ramekins. Bake until custards set, about 30 minutes. Let stand 5 minutes.

Add espresso to remaining custard mixture; stir until dissolved. Spoon espresso custard over white chocolate custards, dividing equally. Bake until custards set, about 30 minutes. Remove from water. Chill uncovered until cold, about 3 hours. *(Can be made 1 day ahead. Cover; keep chilled.)*

Cut around ramekin sides to loosen custards. Turn out onto plates. Serve custards immediately.

6 SERVINGS

Mocha Marble Mousse

◆ ◆ ◆

1   cup milk (do not use low-fat or nonfat)
4   teaspoons instant coffee powder
4   cups miniature marshmallows

2   cups chilled whipping cream
1   teaspoon vanilla extract
7   ounces semisweet chocolate, chopped

Combine milk and coffee powder in heavy medium saucepan. Stir over medium heat until coffee dissolves. Add marshmallows; stir until marshmallows melt and mixture is smooth, about 3 minutes. Pour into large bowl. Let stand at room temperature until cool but not set, whisking occasionally, about 1 hour.

Beat cream and vanilla in medium bowl until stiff peaks form. Fold ½ cup whipped cream into coffee mixture. Fold remaining cream into coffee mixture in 2 additions. Stir chocolate in top of double boiler over simmering water until melted. Turn off heat. Pour melted chocolate into large bowl, reserving 1 tablespoon in top of double boiler for garnish. Cool chocolate to lukewarm. Whisk 1 cup coffee mousse into chocolate in bowl. Gently fold 1 more cup coffee mousse into chocolate mixture. Pour remaining coffee mousse over. Using large spatula, gently swirl to create marbled effect.

Spoon mousse into 6 goblets. Rewarm reserved 1 tablespoon chocolate in top of double boiler over simmering water if necessary. Drizzle chocolate over each dessert. Cover and chill overnight.

6 SERVINGS

◆ ◆ ◆

Melted miniature marshmallows are used to lighten and thicken this creamy mousse. Prepare this dessert a day before you plan to serve it, leaving it time to chill overnight.

◆ ◆ ◆

Chocolate-Hazelnut Mousse

◆ ◆ ◆

½ cup hazelnuts (about 2 ounces), toasted, husked
5 tablespoons sugar
4 ounces bittersweet (not unsweetened) or semisweet chocolate, chopped

3 large eggs, separated
5 tablespoons water
2 tablespoons Frangelico (hazelnut liqueur) or brandy

Pinch of salt

½ cup chilled whipping cream
Additional whipped cream
Additional toasted hazelnuts

Grind ½ cup hazelnuts with 1 tablespoon sugar in processor until mixture forms paste. Set aside. Melt chocolate in small metal bowl set over saucepan of simmering water, stirring until smooth. Remove chocolate from over water.

Whisk egg yolks, 2 tablespoons water, Frangelico and 2 tablespoons sugar in large metal bowl to blend. Set bowl over same saucepan of simmering water and whisk constantly until thick ribbons form when whisk is lifted and thermometer inserted into mixture registers 160°F, about 6 minutes. Cool mixture slightly. Fold in melted chocolate and hazelnut paste.

Using electric mixer, beat egg whites and pinch of salt in large bowl until soft peaks form. Stir remaining 2 tablespoons sugar and 3 tablespoons water in very small saucepan over medium heat until sugar dissolves. Increase heat and boil until thermometer inserted into mixture registers 220°F, about 4 minutes. Gradually add hot syrup to whites, beating until firm peaks form and whites are cool. Fold into chocolate mixture in 2 additions.

Beat ½ cup whipping cream in medium bowl until soft peaks form. Fold into mousse. Spoon mousse into 4 goblets, dividing equally. Chill mousse at least 1 hour and up to 1 day. Garnish each serving with whipped cream and toasted hazelnuts.

4 SERVINGS

Champagne Parfaits with
Pears and Raspberries

❖ ❖ ❖

3 cups dry Champagne or rosé sparkling wine
½ teaspoon unflavored gelatin
1 cup plus 1 tablespoon sugar
2 large firm but ripe pears, peeled, cored, quartered

6 large egg yolks

2 ½-pint baskets raspberries
1 cup chilled whipping cream

4 mint sprigs
12 rose petals from unsprayed roses (optional)

Place 1 tablespoon Champagne in small bowl. Sprinkle gelatin over; let stand until soft, about 10 minutes. Combine remaining Champagne and 1 cup sugar in heavy medium saucepan; stir over medium heat until sugar dissolves. Increase heat and bring to boil. Add pears; reduce heat and simmer just until pears are tender, turning often, about 6 minutes. Using slotted spoon, place pears on plate; cool. Boil liquid until reduced to 1⅓ cups, 15 minutes.

Whisk egg yolks in medium bowl to blend. Gradually whisk in hot poaching liquid; return mixture to same saucepan. Stir over medium-low heat until candy thermometer registers 175°F, about 4 minutes. Remove from heat; add gelatin mixture and whisk until dissolved. Refrigerate custard until thickened but not set, stirring occasionally, approximately 1 hour.

Set aside 4 raspberries for garnish. Combine remaining raspberries and 1 tablespoon sugar in medium bowl. Let stand 10 minutes. Coarsely chop pears. Beat cream until stiff peaks form. Fold cream into custard. Place ¼ cup raspberries in each of four 12- to 16-ounce goblets or balloon-shaped wineglasses. Spoon half of pears over raspberries, dividing equally. Spoon ½ cup custard over each. Repeat layering with remaining berries, pears and custard. Cover with foil; chill until custard is set, at least 6 hours or overnight.

Garnish parfaits with reserved berries, mint and rose petals.

4 SERVINGS

❖ ❖ ❖

There's something wonderfully romantic about this dessert — its velvety texture, the Champagne, the raspberries, even the rose petal garnish. But it has a practical side too, since it can be made a day ahead.

❖ ❖ ❖

Orange Custard with Caramel

◆ ◆ ◆

CUSTARD

2   oranges

2   cups milk (do not use low-fat or nonfat)

1   cup half and half

¾   cup plus 2 tablespoons sugar

1   1-inch piece vanilla bean, split in half lengthwise

4   large eggs

3   large egg yolks

CARAMEL

1¼   cups sugar

¼   cup plus 3 tablespoons water

½   teaspoon fresh lemon juice

3   cups assorted mixed fresh berries

FOR CUSTARD: Using vegetable peeler, cut peel (orange part only) in wide strips from oranges. Combine milk, half and half and sugar in saucepan. Scrape seeds from vanilla bean into milk mixture; add bean. Bring to simmer, stirring until sugar dissolves. Add peel. Remove from heat. Cover and steep 30 minutes.

Strain mixture into medium bowl; cool to lukewarm. Whisk eggs and yolks in large bowl to blend. Gradually whisk milk mixture into eggs. Refrigerate until cold.

FOR CARAMEL: Mix 1 cup sugar, ¼ cup water and juice in heavy medium saucepan. Stir over low heat until sugar dissolves. Increase heat; boil without stirring until syrup turns deep amber, occasionally swirling pan and brushing down sides with wet pastry brush, about 10 minutes. Add 3 tablespoons water (mixture will bubble). Stir over low heat until hard bits dissolve. Immediately pour into 6-cup soufflé dish; swirl to coat bottom and halfway up sides. Cool.

Preheat oven to 350°F. Whisk custard; pour into caramel-coated dish. Place in large baking pan. Fill pan with enough hot water to come halfway up sides of dish. Cover pan completely with foil, sealing at edges. Bake until center 3 inches of custard moves only slightly when dish is shaken, about 1 hour. Remove from oven; let stand covered 10 minutes. Remove from water; chill overnight.

Combine berries and ¼ cup sugar. Let stand 30 minutes. Run knife around sides of dish to loosen custard. Place platter atop dish. Invert custard onto platter. Remove dish; allow caramel to spill out onto platter. Garnish with some berries. Serve, passing remaining berry mixture separately.

8 SERVINGS

Amaretto Chocolate Pudding

◆ ◆ ◆

1   3.4-ounce box (cook and serve) chocolate pudding mix
2   ounces semisweet chocolate, finely chopped
1½ cups plus 2 tablespoons milk
7   tablespoons amaretto liqueur

½   cup chilled whipping cream
1   tablespoon sugar

Pour dry chocolate pudding mix into heavy medium saucepan. Add chopped semisweet chocolate. Gradually mix in milk and 6 tablespoons amaretto liqueur. Stir pudding over medium heat until chocolate melts and pudding comes to boil and thickens. Divide pudding equally among four ¾-cup ramekins or custard cups. Refrigerate until cold, at least 1 hour. *(Can be prepared 1 day ahead. Cover puddings and keep refrigerated.)*

Whip cream, sugar and remaining 1 tablespoon amaretto liqueur in small bowl until stiff peaks form. Top chilled puddings with large dollop of whipped cream.

4 SERVINGS

These elegant *and* easy chocolate puddings would look all the more impressive with a garnish of raspberries and chocolate curls.

◆ ◆ ◆

Chocolate Chip and Ginger
Frozen Yogurt Cake

◆ ◆ ◆

CRUST

1½	cups gingersnap cookie crumbs
1	cup slivered almonds (about 4½ ounces), toasted
¼	cup packed brown sugar
5	tablespoons butter, melted

FILLING

2	pints vanilla frozen yogurt, softened slightly
1	pint chocolate frozen yogurt, softened slightly
6	ounces bittersweet (not unsweetened) or semisweet chocolate, chopped into medium-fine pieces
¼	cup plus 2 tablespoons chopped drained stem ginger in syrup*
3	tablespoons syrup from stem ginger in syrup
6	tablespoons gingersnap cookie crumbs
1	jar purchased hot fudge sauce

FOR CRUST: Preheat oven to 325°F. Butter 9-inch-diameter springform pan with 2¾-inch-high sides. Combine gingersnap crumbs, almonds and brown sugar in processor and grind finely. Mix in butter. Transfer to pan and press crumbs onto bottom and 2 inches up sides. Bake until golden, 12 minutes. Cool on rack.

FOR FILLING: Turn vanilla frozen yogurt into large bowl. Turn chocolate frozen yogurt into medium bowl. Mix ⅔ cup chopped chocolate, ¼ cup ginger and 2 tablespoons ginger syrup into vanilla frozen yogurt. Mix remaining chopped chocolate, 2 tablespoons ginger and 1 tablespoon ginger syrup into chocolate frozen yogurt.

Spread half of vanilla frozen yogurt in crust. Sprinkle with 2 tablespoons gingersnap crumbs. Spread chocolate frozen yogurt over. Sprinkle with 2 tablespoons crumbs. Spread remaining vanilla frozen yogurt over. Smooth top. Sprinkle remaining 2 tablespoons crumbs over. Freeze until firm, at least 2 hours.

Heat hot fudge sauce in heavy small saucepan over low heat until just warm. Drizzle ¼ cup decoratively over top of cake. Cut cake into slices, spooning remaining sauce over each.

*Available at specialty foods stores and some supermarkets.

10 SERVINGS

Frozen yogurt has become the fashionable alternative to ice cream for those who crave the cool without the calories or cholesterol. It has seldom tasted—or looked—better than it does in this dessert (which, by the way, can be made two days ahead of time and kept frozen.)

◆ ◆ ◆

Lemon Macaroon Ice Cream with Blueberry Compote

◆ ◆ ◆

4	lemons
1	cup milk
1	cup sugar
4	large egg yolks
3	cups whipping cream
1	cup crushed amaretti* cookies (Italian macaroons)

Blueberry Compote (see recipe below)

Using vegetable peeler, cut peel (yellow part only) in wide strips from 3 lemons. Finely grate enough peel from remaining lemon to measure 1¼ teaspoons packed peel. Squeeze enough juice from lemon to yield 5 teaspoons. Combine milk and lemon peel strips in medium saucepan and bring to simmer. Remove from heat; cover pan and let steep 20 minutes.

Add sugar to milk mixture. Stir over medium heat until sugar dissolves. Whisk yolks in medium bowl to blend. Gradually whisk in hot milk mixture. Return mixture to same saucepan; stir over low heat until custard coats spoon when finger is drawn across, about 5 minutes (do not boil). Strain into bowl. Whisk in cream, grated lemon peel and lemon juice. Cover; chill until cold.

Freeze custard in ice cream maker. Fold ⅔ cup crushed cookies into ice cream. Cover and store in freezer.

Scoop ice cream into bowls. Spoon warm Blueberry Compote over. Sprinkle with ⅓ cup crushed amaretti cookies.

Available at Italian markets and in some supermarkets.

6 SERVINGS

Blueberry Compote

½	cup plus 2 tablespoons water
½	cup sugar
2½	teaspoons fresh lemon juice
4	cups fresh blueberries or frozen, thawed

Stir water, sugar and juice in saucepan over low heat until sugar dissolves. Add berries; bring to boil. Reduce heat; simmer until mixture thickens slightly, about 2 minutes. Cool slightly.

MAKES ABOUT 4 CUPS

ABOUT AMARETTI

Amaretti—those light-as-air, almond-scented meringue cookies that go so well with a cup of espresso—were invented by the Italians. There are dozens of variations on this classic treat, which is usually made of finely ground almonds and formed in a smooth oval shape. The finest are as small as almonds themselves. Sometimes ground bitter almonds are added for extra flavor.

Amaretti are readily available at supermarkets and Italian markets, usually wrapped in paper in pairs and sold in decorative canisters. Connoisseurs, however, claim that store-bought brands don't begin to capture the sweetness and almond fragrance of homemade amaretti.

◆ ◆ ◆

Blackberry and Hazelnut Sundaes

◆ ◆ ◆

⅓   cup sugar

⅓   cup (packed) golden brown sugar

⅓   cup water

2   tablespoons butter

3   tablespoons Frangelico (hazelnut liqueur) or amaretto

⅓   cup hazelnuts (about 2 ounces), toasted, husked, chopped

   Vanilla frozen yogurt or ice cream

1   ½-pint basket fresh blackberries

Combine sugar, brown sugar and water in heavy small saucepan. Stir over medium-low heat until both sugars dissolve. Add butter and stir until melted. Increase heat and boil until sauce is reduced to ½ cup, about 4 minutes. Remove from heat. Mix in Frangelico and nuts. *(Can be prepared 1 day ahead. Let sauce stand at room temperature. Before using, stir sauce over low heat until heated through and smooth.)*

Scoop frozen yogurt or ice cream into bowls. Spoon warm sauce over. Top with fresh blackberries.

4 SERVINGS

Mango Sorbet

◆ ◆ ◆

2   1-pound mangoes, peeled, pitted, chopped

½   cup sugar

6   tablespoons water

2   tablespoons fresh lime juice

Puree mangoes in processor. Transfer to medium bowl. Mix sugar and water in small saucepan. Stir over medium heat just until sugar dissolves. Stir sugar syrup into mango puree. Stir in lime juice. Refrigerate until cold, about 1 hour.

Transfer mango mixture to ice cream maker and process according to manufacturer's instructions. Transfer sorbet to bowl. Cover sorbet; freeze until firm.

MAKES ABOUT 3 CUPS

For an island touch, serve scoops of this tropical-tasting sorbet with wedges of different melons carved into whimsical leaf shapes.

◆ ◆ ◆

Frozen Framboise Mousse with Apricot Sauce and Raspberries

◆ ◆ ◆

6   egg yolks
½   cup sugar
¼   cup water
3   tablespoons framboise liqueur (raspberry eau de vie)*
1   8-ounce container crème fraîche or sour cream

1   30-ounce can apricots in syrup

1   ½-pint basket fresh raspberries

Whisk yolks, sugar and water in medium metal bowl. Set bowl over saucepan of simmering water (do not allow bottom of bowl to touch water). Whisk until candy thermometer registers 160°F, about 4 minutes. Remove from water. Using electric mixer, beat mixture until cool and thick, about 5 minutes. Beat in framboise. Add crème fraîche; beat just until blended. Divide mixture among six ¾-cup soufflé dishes. Freeze until firm, at least 2 hours or overnight.

Drain apricots, reserving 6 tablespoons syrup. Puree apricots with reserved syrup in processor. Transfer puree to bowl; chill.

Dip soufflé dishes briefly into hot water. Run small knife around sides of each. Wipe dishes dry. Turn out each mousse onto chilled plate. Spoon sauce around mousse. Garnish with berries.

*Available at some liquor stores and specialty foods stores.

6 SERVINGS

Butter Pecan Ice Cream Pie

◆ ◆ ◆

CARAMEL SAUCE

6   tablespoons (¾ stick) unsalted butter

1½ cups (packed) golden brown sugar

¾   cup whipping cream

      Pinch of salt

½   teaspoon vanilla extract

CRUST

⅓   cup (packed) golden brown sugar

¼   cup (½ stick) unsalted butter, room temperature

1   teaspoon vanilla extract

⅔   cup all purpose flour

⅔   cup chopped pecans, lightly toasted

½   gallon butter pecan or almond praline ice cream, softened slightly

36 to 40 pecan halves, toasted (optional)

FOR SAUCE: Melt butter in heavy medium saucepan over medium heat. Add sugar, cream and salt and whisk until sauce is smooth and comes to simmer. Remove from heat; mix in vanilla. Cool sauce completely, stirring occasionally.

FOR CRUST: Preheat oven to 350°F. Butter bottom of 9-inch-diameter springform pan. Using electric mixer, beat brown sugar, butter and vanilla extract in medium bowl until smooth. Add flour and ⅔ cup chopped pecans and stir until moist clumps form. Press dough onto bottom and ½ inch up sides of prepared pan. Bake until crust is set and beginning to brown, about 12 minutes. Cool.

Spoon ice cream into crust, pressing to compact. Pour ½ cup sauce over. Using tip of small knife, swirl sauce and top layer of ice cream, creating marbled pattern. Cover pie and freeze 12 hours. *(Sauce and pie can be prepared 3 days ahead. Cover remaining sauce and refrigerate. Keep pie frozen.)*

Run small sharp knife around pan sides to loosen pie. Release pan sides. Arrange toasted pecan halves decoratively around top edge of pie, if desired. Let pie stand 5 minutes to soften slightly.

Rewarm remaining caramel sauce. Cut ice cream pie into wedges and serve immediately with sauce.

8 TO 10 SERVINGS

A simple nut crust and a smooth caramel sauce are all the preparation required for this impressive dessert. Be sure to start making it at least 12 hours before serving to give it time to freeze; you can prepare the pie up to three days ahead of time.

◆ ◆ ◆

Pineapple Split

◆ ◆ ◆

1   cup tropical, mango, guava or papaya fruit nectar

½   cup sugar

1   fresh pineapple, peeled, halved lengthwise, cored, each half cut crosswise into 9 half-moon slices

1½ pints (about) tropical-flavored sorbet (such as mango, banana, coconut or pineapple)

1   cup shredded sweetened coconut, toasted
     Fresh mint sprigs

Stir nectar and sugar in heavy medium saucepan over high heat until sugar dissolves and syrup comes to boil. Boil until syrup is reduced to ⅔ cup, about 5 minutes. Cool syrup completely (syrup will thicken as it cools). *(Can be prepared 1 day ahead. Cover and let stand at room temperature.)*

Overlap 3 pineapple slices to form ring on each of 6 plates. Place 1 scoop sorbet in center of each ring. Drizzle syrup over, then sprinkle generously with coconut. Garnish with mint.

6 SERVINGS

ICES, GRANITAS AND SORBETS

While ice cream is a known product, some of the other frozen desserts available now are less familiar. Here's a brief guide to what's what.

- Frappé: A sherbet or sorbet that has been whipped or pressed through a sieve while partly frozen for a slightly slushy, frothy texture.
- Granita: Similar to sorbet but frozen in a metal pan or bowl and occasionally stirred for a coarser, more granular texture.
- Ice: Made of fruit juice, sugar and water and frozen in an ice cream machine, ices are less intensely flavored than sorbets.
- Sherbet: Fruit puree mixed with a little milk, egg white or gelatin for smoothness and body, and then frozen in a machine.
- Sorbet: Like ices, though more intense in taste, sometimes flavored with a liqueur.

◆ ◆ ◆

Coffee Granita

◆ ◆ ◆

1½   cups water
1   cup sugar
¾   cup brewed espresso coffee or ¾ cup very hot water mixed with 2 tablespoons instant espresso powder

½   cup chilled whipping cream, whipped

Stir water and sugar in heavy medium saucepan over medium heat until sugar dissolves and syrup boils 1 minute. Cool syrup. Mix in coffee. Pour mixture into medium-size metal bowl. Freeze until ice mixture is solid, about 3 hours.

Using fork, scrape ice to form flakes. Return to freezer; keep frozen until ready to serve.

Pile coffee granita into stemmed glasses. Top with generous amounts of whipped cream and serve.

4 SERVINGS

Red, White and Blueberry Sundaes

◆ ◆ ◆

1   cup orange juice
7   tablespoons Grand Marnier or other orange liqueur
6   tablespoons sugar
5   tablespoons unsalted butter

2   nectarines, halved, pitted, cut into ½-inch wedges
1⅓   cups blueberries
1⅓   cups sliced hulled strawberries

1½   pints (about) vanilla ice cream or frozen yogurt
     Mint leaves

Combine orange juice, Grand Marnier, sugar and butter in heavy large skillet. Stir over medium-high heat until sugar dissolves and sauce comes to simmer. Simmer until sauce thickens slightly and is reduced to 1 cup, about 10 minutes.

Add nectarines to sauce and toss until heated through, about 2 minutes. Add blueberries and strawberries; toss fruit mixture until heated through, about 1 minute.

Divide fruit mixture among 6 dessert bowls. Place 1 scoop ice cream in center of fruit. Garnish with mint.

6 SERVINGS

Honey Phyllo Ice Cream Cups

◆ ◆ ◆

CUPS

Nonstick vegetable oil spray

9   tablespoons (½ stick plus 1 tablespoon) unsalted butter
3   tablespoons honey
5   sheets fresh phyllo pastry or frozen, thawed
    (each about 12 x 18 inches)

TOPPING

⅓   cup honey
2   tablespoons fresh lemon juice

1½ pints (about) vanilla, strawberry or peach ice cream or
    frozen yogurt
    Assorted berries or thinly sliced peaches

FOR CUPS: Preheat oven to 375°F. Spray 2 heavy large baking sheets with nonstick vegetable oil spray. Arrange three ¾-cup ramekins or custard cups upside down on each baking sheet, spacing evenly. Spray outside of ramekins with vegetable oil spray.

Stir butter and honey in small saucepan over low heat just until butter melts and mixture is smooth. Place 1 phyllo sheet on work surface (cover remainder with plastic and damp towel). Brush butter mixture over sheet. Cut sheet into six 6-inch squares. Stack 5 squares, with points of each going in different directions (reserve 1 square for next cup). Lift stack; place stack, buttered side down, on 1 ramekin. Press stack firmly, molding to ramekin. Repeat buttering, cutting, stacking and shaping with remaining phyllo, using 5 squares for each stack and making a total of 6 cups. Brush outside of phyllo with butter mixture.

Bake until phyllo is brown and crisp, about 14 minutes. Immediately run spatula under edges of phyllo to loosen. Transfer baking sheets to racks; cool 10 minutes. Slide spatula under phyllo and ramekins and lift from baking sheet. Remove phyllo from ramekins and place upright on baking sheets; cool completely. *(Can be prepared 3 hours ahead. Let stand at room temperature.)*

FOR TOPPING: Whisk honey and lemon juice in small bowl.

Place phyllo cups on plates. Place 1 scoop ice cream in each. Spoon fruit around ice cream. Drizzle with topping.

6 SERVINGS

◆ COOKIES ◆

Strawberry Stacks

◆ ◆ ◆

1   cup all purpose flour
6   tablespoons sugar
1   teaspoon grated orange peel
¼   teaspoon salt
¼   cup (½ stick) chilled unsalted butter, cut into pieces
2   tablespoons chilled solid vegetable shortening
1   tablespoon orange juice

    Whipping cream

1   1-pint basket strawberries, hulled, quartered
1   tablespoon Grand Marnier or other orange liqueur
1   cup chilled whipping cream
2   teaspoons vanilla extract
4   small strawberries

Mix flour, 2 tablespoons sugar, orange peel and salt in medium bowl. Add butter and shortening and rub in, using fingertips, until mixture resembles coarse meal. Sprinkle orange juice over. Stir with fork until moist clumps form. Gather dough into ball; flatten into disk. Wrap in plastic and refrigerate 30 minutes. *(Can be made 2 days ahead. Keep chilled. Soften slightly before rolling out.)*

Preheat oven to 375°F. Butter heavy large baking sheet. Roll out dough on lightly floured surface to scant ¼-inch-thick round. Using 3-inch round cookie cutter, cut out rounds. Reroll scraps and cut out additional rounds, forming 8 total. Transfer rounds to prepared baking sheet. Brush lightly with cream. Sprinkle with 1 tablespoon sugar, dividing equally. Bake cookies until light golden brown, about 15 minutes. Cool on baking sheet on rack.

Combine quartered strawberries, 2 tablespoons sugar and Grand Marnier in medium bowl. Beat 1 cup cream, vanilla and 1 tablespoon sugar in another medium bowl until soft peaks form.

Place 1 cookie on each of 4 plates. Top cookies with berry mixture, dividing equally and allowing mixture to spill over sides of cookies. Spoon large dollops of whipped cream over. Top each with second cookie. Garnish tops with small dollops of whipped cream and whole strawberries. Serve immediately.

4 SERVINGS

No-Fail Chocolate Chippers

◆ ◆ ◆

2 cups old-fashioned rolled oats
1¾ cups all purpose flour
1 teaspoon baking soda
½ teaspoon salt

½ cup (1 stick) butter, room temperature
1 cup (packed) golden brown sugar
½ cup sugar
2 large eggs
1 teaspoon vanilla extract
1 cup chopped walnuts
1 11.5-ounce package (about 2 cups) milk chocolate chips

Preheat oven to 375°F. Finely grind oats in processor. Add flour, baking soda and salt and blend 5 seconds.

Beat butter and both sugars in large bowl until well blended. Beat in eggs and vanilla extract. Mix in dry ingredients. Mix in chopped walnuts and milk chocolate chips.

For each cookie, form 2 rounded tablespoons dough into ball and place on ungreased baking sheet; flatten slightly. Bake until edges are golden brown, about 12 minutes. Cool on sheets 5 minutes. Transfer to racks; cool completely.

MAKES ABOUT 2 DOZEN

Orange and Cinnamon Biscotti

◆ ◆ ◆

1	cup sugar
½	cup (1 stick) unsalted butter, room temperature
2	large eggs
2	teaspoons grated orange peel
1	teaspoon vanilla extract
2	cups all purpose flour
1½	teaspoons baking powder
1	teaspoon ground cinnamon
¼	teaspoon salt

Preheat oven to 325°F. Butter 2 baking sheets. Beat sugar and butter in large bowl until blended. Add eggs 1 at a time, beating well after each. Beat in orange peel and vanilla. Stir flour, baking powder, cinnamon and salt into medium bowl. Add dry ingredients to butter mixture; mix just until incorporated.

Divide dough in half. Place each half on prepared sheet. With lightly floured hands, form each half into 3-inch-wide by ¾-inch-high log. Bake until dough logs are firm to touch, about 35 minutes. Remove dough logs from oven and cool 10 minutes.

Transfer logs to work surface. Using serrated knife, cut on diagonal into ½-inch-thick slices. Arrange cut side down on baking sheets. Bake until bottoms are golden, about 12 minutes. Turn biscotti over; bake until bottoms are golden, about 12 minutes longer. Transfer to racks and cool. *(Can be made 2 weeks ahead. Store in airtight container at room temperature.)*

MAKES ABOUT 2 DOZEN

◆ ◆ ◆

The popularity of biscotti doesn't seem to end. These crunchy Italian cookies, which are neither too rich nor too sweet, are the perfect finale to a contemporary meal, such as the pasta menu on page 123. Serve them with sliced pears and Vin Santo, an Italian dessert wine.

◆ ◆ ◆

Ginger-Macadamia Brownies

◆ ◆ ◆

¾	cup (1½ sticks) unsalted butter, cut into pieces
4	ounces unsweetened chocolate, chopped
1	teaspoon instant coffee powder
3	large eggs
1½	cups (packed) brown sugar
2	teaspoons vanilla extract
¼	teaspoon salt

1   cup unbleached all purpose flour
1   cup chopped macadamia nuts
¼   cup minced crystallized ginger

Preheat oven to 325°F. Butter 8 x 8 x 2-inch glass baking dish. Mix butter, chocolate and coffee powder in heavy medium saucepan. Stir over low heat until smooth. Cool, stirring occasionally.

Whisk eggs in large bowl to blend. Whisk in sugar, vanilla and salt. Fold in chocolate mixture. Mix in flour, then nuts and ginger. Pour batter into prepared pan. Bake until tester inserted into center comes out with moist crumbs still attached, about 40 minutes. Cool in pan on rack. Cover and let stand at room temperature overnight. Cut into 16 squares.

MAKES 16

Sesame-Almond Macaroons

◆ ◆ ◆

½   cup plus 1 tablespoon raw sesame seeds (about 3 ounces)

1   7-ounce package almond paste, broken into small pieces
½   cup sugar
2   large egg whites

Preheat oven to 325°F. Sprinkle sesame seeds on large baking sheet. Place in oven; toast until light golden, stirring occasionally, about 20 minutes. Cool completely.

Line 2 heavy large baking sheets with foil. Butter and flour foil. Using electric mixer, beat almond paste and sugar until only very small pieces of almond paste remain. Add egg whites and mix on high speed until mixture is smooth, about 5 minutes. Mix in toasted sesame seeds. Drop cookie dough by rounded teaspoonfuls onto prepared baking sheets, spacing 2 inches apart.

Bake cookies until puffed, pale golden and edges begin to brown, about 14 minutes. Transfer foil with cookies to rack and cool completely. Carefully peel cookies from foil. *(Can be made 2 days ahead. Store in airtight containers.)*

MAKES ABOUT 36

◆ ◆ ◆

A sophisticated cookie for sesame lovers, and the ideal crunch to accompany a fruit dessert, such as the Pink Grapefruit with Cassis on page 180. Save the extras for afternoon tea or coffee.

◆ ◆ ◆

White Chocolate and Pecan Brownies

3 ounces unsweetened chocolate, chopped

¾ cup (1½ sticks) unsalted butter, room temperature

½ cup firmly packed golden brown sugar

½ cup sugar

3 large eggs

¾ cup all purpose flour

6 ounces white chocolate, cut into ¾-inch pieces

1 cup coarsely chopped pecans

Powdered sugar

Preheat oven to 350°F. Line bottom of 13 x 9 x 2-inch baking pan with aluminum foil. Butter and flour foil and sides of pan. Stir unsweetened chocolate in double boiler set over simmering water until chocolate melts. Remove from over water and cool.

Using electric mixer, beat butter in large bowl until light and fluffy. Gradually add brown sugar and ½ cup sugar and beat until well blended. Mix in melted chocolate. Add eggs 1 at a time and beat just until blended after each addition. Mix in flour. Using rubber spatula, mix in white chocolate and pecans. Transfer to prepared pan.

Bake brownies until tester inserted into center comes out with a few crumbs attached, about 20 minutes. Cool in pan on rack.

Cut around pan sides to loosen brownies. Turn out onto work surface. Peel off foil. Cut into 2- to 3-inch squares. Arrange right side up on plate. Dust with powdered sugar.

MAKES ABOUT 32

Orange Blossom Almond Crescents

◆ ◆ ◆

PASTRY

2   cups all purpose flour

¼   teaspoon salt

1   cup (2 sticks) chilled unsalted butter, cut into small pieces

¼   cup (about) ice water

FILLING

½   cup blanched almonds, toasted

1   7-ounce package almond paste

¼   cup unsalted butter, room temperature

2   tablespoons sugar

1   large egg

3   tablespoons orange flower water*

½   cup powdered sugar

FOR PASTRY: Combine flour and salt in large bowl. Add butter and rub with fingertips until mixture resembles coarse meal. Add enough ice water by tablespoonfuls just to bind dough, tossing with fork. Divide into 2 pieces. Lightly dust dough with flour; flatten each piece into rectangle. Wrap and chill at least 1 hour.

FOR FILLING: Finely grind almonds in processor. Add almond paste, butter, 2 tablespoons sugar, egg and 1 tablespoon orange flower water. Process until smooth. Transfer to bowl; chill 1 hour.

Position rack in center of oven and preheat to 400°F. Roll out 1 pastry rectangle on lightly floured surface to 13x15-inch rectangle. Trim to 12-inch square. Cut into sixteen 3-inch squares. Place 1 teaspoon almond filling ½ inch from 1 corner of 1 pastry square. Beginning at same corner, roll corner of dough tightly over filling and continue rolling as for jelly roll. Pinch ends firmly to seal in filling. Gently shape into crescent. Place crescent on large baking sheet. Repeat with remaining dough squares and filling. Roll, cut, fill and shape remaining pastry rectangle. Bake until golden brown, about 20 minutes. Cool pastries slightly.

While pastries are still warm, brush lightly with remaining 2 tablespoons orange flower water. Turn pastries 1 at a time in powdered sugar to coat. Transfer to rack and cool completely. *(Can be made 1 day ahead. Store in airtight container at room temperature.)*

* A flavoring extract available at liquor stores and in the liquor or specialty foods sections of some supermarkets.

MAKES 32

◆ ◆ ◆

These tender, filled pastries have an almond paste center and are lightly scented with orange flower water, a wonderfully fragrant flavoring extract. Try them with the Perfumed Oranges on page 185.

◆ ◆ ◆

Chocolate Drop Cookies

◆ ◆ ◆

2   cups all purpose flour
½   teaspoon baking soda
½   teaspoon salt
½   cup vegetable shortening
2   ounces unsweetened chocolate, chopped
1   cup firmly packed golden brown sugar
1   large egg
½   cup sour cream
1   teaspoon vanilla extract

Chocolate Icing (see recipe on page 219)

Preheat oven to 350°F. Grease 2 heavy large baking sheets. Sift 2 cups flour, ½ teaspoon baking soda and ½ teaspoon salt into medium bowl. Stir ½ cup vegetable shortening and unsweetened chocolate in heavy small saucepan over low heat until chocolate melts and mixture is smooth. Transfer mixture to large bowl. Cool slightly. Add 1 cup brown sugar and beat until blended. Add egg and beat until blended. Stir in dry ingredients, then ½ cup sour cream and 1 teaspoon vanilla extract. Drop cookie batter by tablespoonfuls onto prepared baking sheets, spacing evenly.

Bake until cookies feel firm to touch, about 10 minutes. Transfer cookies to racks and cool. Drizzle warm icing over cookies.

MAKES 3 DOZEN

Chocolate Icing

¼ cup coffee
1½ ounces unsweetened chocolate, chopped
1¾ cups powdered sugar, sifted

Stir coffee and chopped chocolate in heavy medium saucepan over low heat until chocolate melts and mixture is smooth. Remove from heat. Whisk in powdered sugar. Use immediately.

MAKES ABOUT ¾ CUP

Sugar Cookies

◆ ◆ ◆

½ cup (1 stick) butter, room temperature
½ cup vegetable oil
½ cup sugar
½ cup powdered sugar
1 egg
1 teaspoon vanilla extract
2¼ cups all purpose flour
½ teaspoon baking soda
½ teaspoon cream of tartar
½ teaspoon salt

   Additional sugar

Using electric mixer, beat butter, oil, ½ cup sugar and ½ cup powdered sugar in large bowl until well blended. Mix in egg and vanilla. Sift flour, baking soda, cream of tartar and salt over and mix in. Cover; chill until firm, about 30 minutes or up to 1 day.

Preheat oven to 350°F. Butter 2 heavy large baking sheets. Roll 1 tablespoon dough into ball. Place on prepared sheet. Repeat with remaining dough, spacing balls evenly on sheets. Dip flat-bottomed glass into water to moisten, then dip into sugar and press dough to ¼-inch-thick round. Repeat with remaining dough balls, dipping bottom of glass into sugar before pressing each.

Bake cookies until light brown, about 15 minutes. Transfer cookies to racks and cool completely.

MAKES ABOUT 36

◆ ◆ ◆

These cookies are simple to prepare and delicious to eat — a favorite with young and old alike. For variety, try adding one-half cup dried currants or chopped nuts to the dough.

◆ ◆ ◆

·Index·

Acknowledgments

The following people contributed the recipes included in this book: A Pacific Cafe, Kapaa, Kauai, Hawaii; Mary Barber; Melanie Barnard; Rosie Bialowas; Lena Cederham Birnbaum; Penelope Casas; Sara Corpening; Cottage Inn, Eureka Springs, Arkansas; Lane Crowther; Gretchen Davis; Tony DiSalvo; Brooke Dojny; Don Camillo, Nice, France; Dorothy Duder; Carol Field; Janet Fletcher; Lucy Footlik; Four Seasons Resort Bali, Bali, Indonesia; Cheryl Gavard-Heinmiller; Joël Guillet; Janie Hibler; Ginny Leith Holland; The Hotel Hershey, Hershey, Pennsylvania; Karen Kaplan; Shari Kaplan; Barbara Karoff; Kedron Valley Inn, South Woodstock, Vermont; Jeanne Thiel Kelley; Kristine Kidd; Elinor Klivans; Diane Kochilas; Aglaia Kremezi; Le Bistrot du Port, Nice, France; Le Chat Grippé, Paris, France; Le Safari, Nice, France; Sarabeth Levine; Lou Balico, Nice, France; Ron Maiberg; Tess Mallos; March, New York, New York; Sheila and Bill McCaffery; Michael McLaughlin; Alice Medrich; Jinx and Jefferson Morgan; Selma Brown Morrow; Kitty Morse; Norma at the Wharfhouse, St. James, Jamaica, West Indies; Beatrice Ojakangas; The Palmer House Inn, Falmouth, Massachusetts; Neela Paniz; The Rapids Lodge, Grand Lake, Colorado; Restaurant Bruneau, Brussels, Belgium; Claudia Roden; Betty Rosbottom; Roy's Poipu Bar & Grill, Poipu, Kauai, Hawaii; Richard Sax; Martha Rose Shulman; Marie Simmons; Marlena Spieler; Dimitris and Sofia Stamos; Kevin Taylor; Michael Thompson; Mary Jo Thoresen; Marimar Torres; Charlotte Walker; Joanne Weir; Clifford A. Wright; Zenith American Grill, Denver, Colorado.

The following people contributed the photographs included in this book: Jack Andersen; David Bishop; Viktor Budnik; Ed Carey; Wyatt Counts; Deborah Denker; Julie Dennis; Mark Ferri; Beth Galton; Tony Giammarino; Henry Hamamoto; Jim Hansen; Image Company/Heinz Troll; Charles Imstepf; Mark Laita; Brian Leatart; Michael Luppino; Andrew Martin; Drew Meredith; Graham Monro; Gary Moss; Judd Pilossof; Jeff Sarpa; Margaret Skinner; Mark Thomas; Tim Turner; Gianni Ummarino/Franca Speranza; Bruce Van Inwegen; Georges Véron; Elizabeth Zeschin.

Front jacket photo: David Bishop, Photographer; Roscoe Betsill, Food Stylist; Randi Barritt, Prop Stylist.